EVEN MORE FOR YOUR GARDEN

Books by

V. SACKVILLE-WEST

Poetry

THE LAND
KING'S DAUGHTER
COLLECTED POEMS
SOLITUDE
THE GARDEN

Biography and Criticism

THE EAGLE AND THE DOVE
PEPITA
ANDREW MARVELL
APHRA BEHN
SAINT JOAN OF ARC

Travel

PASSENGER TO TEHERAN
TWELVE DAYS

Miscellaneous

SOME FLOWERS
COUNTRY NOTES
COUNTRY NOTES IN WARTIME
KNOLE AND THE SACKVILLES
NURSERY RHYMES
IN YOUR GARDEN
IN YOUR GARDEN AGAIN
MORE FOR YOUR GARDEN

Fiction

THE EDWARDIANS
ALL PASSION SPENT
GRAND CANYON
THE EASTER PARTY

V. SACKVILLE-WEST

Even More For Your Garden

FRANCES LINCOLN

FRANCES LINCOLN LTD
4 Torriano Mews
Torriano Avenue
London NW5 2RZ
www.franceslincoln.com

First published by
MICHAEL JOSEPH LTD 1958

EVEN MORE FOR YOUR GARDEN

A CIP catalogue record for this book is available from the British Library.

First Frances Lincoln Edition 2004

ISBN 0 7112 2357 2

Printed in England

2 4 6 8 9 7 5 3 1

Foreword

THIS is the fourth collection to be published in book form of articles contributed weekly to *The Observer*.

This series covers the dates from April 8, 1955, to October 6, 1957—roughly, another two years' worth.

I often get reproached by readers of *The Observer* for recommending plants they say they can't find in any catalogue. This is not my fault. *The Observer* cannot allow me to mention names and addresses of nurserymen, thus giving a free advertisement. In this book, however, as in the three previous volumes, I have appended a list of nurserymen, pp. 195–199, from whom you should be able to obtain anything you want.

I must for the fourth time thank *The Observer* not only for continuing to employ me, but also for allowing me to reprint these articles.

V. S.-W.

Sissinghurst Castle, Kent.

Contents

Index of Plants

EVEN MORE FOR YOUR GARDEN

January

January 1, 1956

IT might be agreeable to start the year with a consideration of scents, a mysterious and alluring subject suggested to me by the queer behaviour of two pots of
Persian cyclamen I had raised from seed of a specially
selected sweet-scented strain. They smelt delicious in the
greenhouse and I carried them triumphantly indoors. All
trace of scent disappeared, but that might be attributed to
the change of temperature, of the degree of moisture in the
air, and even a relative lack of light. Two days later, however, the whole room was fragrant, but—mark this—the
fragrance emanated from only one of the two pots. Next
day the situation was reversed: the plant that had been
scentless was now doing all that could be wished of it, and
the other wasn't.

So it has gone on. Identical twins could not be living
under more identical conditions, yet they continue to choose
different days and different hours of the day for their per-
formance. Why?

We know that we owe our pleasure in flower-scent to
certain essential oils contained in cells which release their
content by some process not fully understood. The essential
oils are what we call attars, one of the few words for which
the English language has to thank the Persian. (Attar of
roses will be the most familiar to most people.) The chemical
composition of these attars has been analysed, and you
would be surprised to learn what everyday substances we

should encounter if we were to take some favourite petals to pieces, alcohol for instance, vinegar, benzine; but I am no chemist and should blunder into some shocking howlers were I to pursue the subject. I profess to be nothing more than the average gardener, enjoying such useless but charming bits of information as that some butterflies and moths exude the same scent as the flowers they visit; that white flowers are the most numerous among the scented kinds, followed by red, yellow, and purple in that order, with blue a very bad fifth; that flowers fertilized by birds have no scent at all, birds being without a sense of smell; that dark-haired people have the most highly developed sense, whereas albinos are generally lacking it altogether; that some flowers smell different in the morning from in the evening; and, finally, that the flower-like scent so often observed emanating from the dead bodies of saintly persons may be due to the same breaking-down or release of essential oils in the first stages of decomposition. This supposedly mystical fragrance is usually said to suggest roses or violets.

None of this, however, explains the peculiar conduct of my two pots of cyclamen.

January 6, 1957

Oh dear, I often say to myself as I sit down to this weekly article, what thin rubbish I do write—I really feel ashamed, sometimes, of the poor fare I supply. I would like it to be all rich and bejewelled and redolent as the gifts brought by the Kings on this day of Epiphany. Surely with a subject so extensive as all the range of flowers over a vast world I ought to be able to weave a tapestry worthy of such a creation.

As it is, on this first Sunday of the year, I can think only of the sombre conifer.

Some people like conifers; I, frankly, don't. That may sound too sweeping. Nobody could be so foolish as not to admire the great dark benedictory arms of *Pinus insignis*; the sunset-catching trunk of the Scots pine; or the Italian cypress; or the tall exclamation mark of *Libocedrus decurrens*, to mention but a few. I must recognize also that they do provide effective contrasts in a garden, and have an architectural value when they are properly placed, but this usually implies a large garden and certainly an old garden where they have had years to reach a dignified maturity. What I think I mean is that I don't like dusty, rusty specimens of, say, *thuya* stuck meaninglessly into the middle of a lawn when that lawn would have looked much happier left peacefully to itself.

Nor have I ever made up my mind about those little obelisks of gloom that many people favour in their rockeries. I suppose there is something to be said for the juniper *communis compressa*, which will scarcely reach two feet in height during its planter's lifetime, but does it not savour too much of those artificially dwarfed trees beloved of the Japanese? They may look all right in Japan, but somehow to my mind they look all wrong in our country, where we are accustomed to trees far exceeding our own stature.

Trees should be noble. Even the Irish juniper *J. fastigiata*, long before attaining its full height of 20 ft. or so, invests its slender column with an adolescent dignity. In fact, there is much to be said for many of the junipers, whether you fancy the blackish-green or the bluish-green, which in some lights is glaucous as a rock-pool; and not the least thing in their favour, from the point of view of people who have to garden on a limy soil, is that they not only tolerate alkalinity, but positively prefer it.

January 8, 1956

I once wrote what seemed to me a spate of articles about soils, acid or alkaline. I thought I had perhaps overdone it, but the importance of the subject justified me, for there can be few things more vital to the well-being of any plant than the soil it has to live in, and also, I might add, to the way it gets looked after immediately after its planting. I could make up a long, sad story about the things I have lost, owing to neglect, forgetfulness, lack of strong staking to stop them from getting root-loosened by wind, and drought ensuing even in the autumn months of October and November when we might expect rain to pour down from heaven.

I now get a letter asking for an article about gardening on clay, a problem which doubtless confronts many people. It confronted me for fifteen years in the first garden I ever had, so I feel I learnt quite a lot, and learnt it bitterly. Let me be frank: it is a dire, plaguy, baleful, thankless soil, workable for about five days out of the year, and for the remaining 360 best described by the dictionary definition as 'a tenacious paste capable of being moulded into any shape, which hardens when dried and forms the material for bricks, tiles, etc.' This may be all right for the sculptor and the builder, but not for the gardener. The stuff is either so sticky that you cannot dig it, or so hard that you can break it only with a mattock, nor is there very much that can be done about it. Lime helps quite a lot, by breaking it up, and so does rough digging in autumn, leaving the clods to be crumbled by winter frosts. Wood-ash lightens it; and if you know how to build a smother-fire or can get a countryman to build one for you, when it should smoulder for days if properly constructed, you will find the resultant heap of burnt clay very useful. But, honestly, clay is a noxious thing.

By way of consolation, people will tell you that roses love it. I found that this was true; my rose bushes were long lived and vigorous. Of course we gave them a good start by incorporating some leaf-mould and peat; it is better to incorporate than to dig out a hole and fill it with the good mixture, as a hole will merely act as a bucket from which the water cannot escape. I found also that syringa (lilacs) did very well, and so did lupins, and for a further consolation I may add that colour seemed to be intensified, but having said that, there is really very little counsel to be given, except to remove your dwelling as speedily as possible to another place.

January 13, 1957

Two days after this article appears, its writer will be on a ship on her way to Indonesia. An odd combination of circumstances is sending me off to this opposite side of the world. I do not know what to expect to find there. Friends tell me that there are hedges of orchids, and that I shall be able to pick bunches of orchids even as I could pick honeysuckle in an English lane.

I wonder whether I can believe this, or whether I should like to, even if I could?

It is an exciting experience to go off into such an unknown climate as the tropics. What will one see, or find, or discover? Will one be envious of such exotic growth, flowering naturally instead of in a greenhouse or displayed in florists' shops? I have always admired the plant hunters who at the risk of their limbs and lives struggled up remote mountains, crossed torrents on a bridge apparently made of two lianas twisted together, hauled themselves up crevices to investigate an inaccessible plant, endured every extreme of cold and heat, drought and rain, hid for days in caves to escape the pursuit of brigands, lay with broken leg on a narrow cliff path while a convoy of fifty mules stepped over the prostrate body, and yet managed to press specimens between sheets of blotting paper and to collect seeds and bulbs for eventual dispatch home.

It is to these valiant and determined creatures that we owe so many of the treasures of our gardens, now taken so much for granted that we casually choose what we want from a nurseryman's catalogue. A postal order for 7s. 6d. returns in the form of a neatly straw-packed bundle. How often do we stop to consider what the discovery and acquisition of that plant has meant to some intrepid man? I wonder also how many amateur gardeners realize that brave young botanists still set out on similar expeditions, partially financed by subscriptions from garden lovers eager to take the chance of receiving a share of the booty.

Particulars of such expeditions and subscriptions would be provided on application to the Royal Horticultural Society, Vincent Square, London, S.W.1.

No such romantic or productive adventure will be mine, and I write this note chiefly to apologize in advance to any *Observer* correspondents who may have to wait for two months before receiving a reply. I usually try to answer letters by return of post, but I can't do that from somewhere in the vicinity of the South China Sea.

January 15, 1956

A reader wants suggestions about how to enliven a 'flat, dull privet hedge,' and I dare say that there are a good many people who would be glad to transform an uninteresting hedge into a thing of comparative beauty. There is no inherent difficulty so long as you bear two facts in mind. The first is that every hedge, privet or otherwise, is a robber of the soil; its intricate web of roots demands sustenance and moisture, with consequent deprivation of any competing occupants.

The moral is obvious: you must feed as richly as possible by top-dressings of whatever good food you can get hold of, whether it be organic or inorganic manuring, to compensate the plunder and pillage and spoliation going on all the time beneath the ground. The second fact is that your hedge will have to be clipped annually, and clipped severely; therefore

you must choose your ramblers and climbers from the
category of plants that does not mind being chopped about
by shears, possibly at quite the wrong time of year.

After all this cautionary preamble I shall be expected to
suggest some real toughs. I think I would plant *Clematis
montana*, either the ordinary white kind or its pale pink
variety *rubra*. This seems to survive any cruelty. Then I
would have wistaria, either the ordinary mauve or the more
exquisite white, both such strong growers that although
they would not get any very expert pruning or spurring
back but would just get slaughtered in a way to make any
professional gardener scream in his sleep, would still prosper
and perhaps be all the better for it. Then I would have
some of the autumn-colouring vines, the magnificent huge-
leaved *coignettiae*, for instance, bright pink in September;
or *Vitis vinifera brandt*, carrying bunches of small black
grapes; and I should certainly have two or three of the
twining *Celastrus orbiculatus*, which isn't much to look at
during the summer but which surprises us with its red-and-
yellow clusters of fruit in October, and is invaluable for
picking as it lasts for weeks and weeks indoors.

The disadvantage of the vines and the *Celastrus* would
be the necessity of leaving the hedge-clipping till rather
late in the year, but I can't see why one should be tied to
the calendar for clipping such nasty hedges as privet. They
are indestructible whatever you do, short of taking a bull-
dozer to root them out, so why not leave them until later
than the orthodox date? I am all for playing rough with
things that play rough with us, and for making them
behave as our servants, not our masters. And so I think that
if you are afflicted with a flat, dull hedge you should take
no notice at all of the time of year the books tell you to cut,
but should regard it merely as a host to the lovelier guests
you wish to weave through it.

January 20, 1957

Argument still rages in the horticultural world about the best time of year to prune roses. According to the old orthodox theory, the time to do it was in the second half of March or in early April. Present-day opinion veers more and more strongly in favour of winter pruning. I don't pretend to be an expert, so please disregard my advice if you disagree with it, but it seems to me common sense to cut the plant when it is dormant, rather than when the sap has begun to rise and must necessarily bleed from the wound.

I know that there are objections. People say 'Oh, but if you prune your roses in December or January, they may start to make fresh growth in the mild weather we sometimes get in late February or early March, and then comes an iron frost and then what happens to those young tender shoots you have encouraged by your precipitate pruning?'

All I can say in answer to that is that you will just have to go over your roses again and cut away all the frost-damaged shoots back to a new eye lower down the stem. You might have to do the same thing after a March pruning, so you will not have lost any time, and on the whole I am on the side of the winter-pruners.

*   *   *   *

Pruning is such a controversial subject that I approach it with diffidence, but of one thing I am sure: it pays always to clear the dead wood out of any shrub. What a tangled mess accumulates at the base of an old bush of philadelphus! What a lot of useless twigs clutter the lilacs! Take your saw and your secateurs, and give a breathing space, especially in the centre. Let the light in, and the air. This advice is of general application, for there is no shrub that will not benefit. Terrified though we may be of cutting inexpertly into living wood, or of cutting at the wrong time, the most

inexperienced amongst us need have no fear in chopping
away dead rubbish which Nature herself has discarded. The
same applies to those little feeble twiggy growths which will
never come to anything and only rob the branch by their
small but cumulative filching of the plant's life. Shave them
off. Weaklings must be sacrificed, in the hard harsh law of
Nature.

January 22, 1956

Gardeners appear to entertain only two attitudes towards
compost: either they swear by it or else they will have
nothing to say to it. Maybe they cannot be bothered, maybe
they mistrust it, asserting that the compost heap brings a
crop of weeds from the buried seeds; at the back of their
minds I suspect they think a bonfire saves a lot of trouble.
Leaf-mould is all very well; leaves have got to be swept up
and barrowed away somewhere, and it is a simple matter
to stack them in a wire enclosure and just let them rot.
Composting demands a little more effort, both in the collecting of the material, the sandwich-like structure of the
heap, the use of activators and neutralizers, the control of
moisture. Still, I fancy that anyone who has once enjoyed
the luxury of slicing his spade into a cake of really rich dark
crumbly compost will feel that he has earned his reward.

He will have obtained something of more nutritive value
than peat, and moreover he will have obtained it for nothing. He will have been spared all the cost of buying fertilizers, excellent and useful though some of those fertilizers
may be. He will have a certain satisfaction in knowing that
he has returned to his soil a great part of what he has taken
from it, and has returned it by a natural method. To any
good gardener, this thought should be a special and seemly
pleasure.

The objection about weed-seeds must be instantly dis-
missed for two reasons. One reason is that the weeds

supplying an important contribution to the green-stuff in the heap can be thrown on to it before they have reached the seeding stage; and the second reason is that the heat generated in any properly constructed heap should suffice to cook any seed into collapse. Temperatures up to 160 deg. Fahrenheit are soon generated. I add this comment, because some employers of stuffy-minded professional gardeners may have come up against the concrete-wall of obstinacy erected against any method regarded as new-fangled; yet, if they only knew, those dear old plodders, we are only asking them to go back to what Nature herself arranged, in her system of decaying vegetation and worms and bacteria, all working together in the production of what we call humus.

If anybody wants to know more about how to make a compost heap, let him study some book about it. I have just been reading one. *Practical Organic Gardening*, by Ben Easey (Faber and Faber, 21s.). It has taught me a lot, and has also given me some good laughs about what you can put on to your compost heap and what you can't.

Apart from the orthodox ingredients, you can put dead snakes, mildewed haggis, burst cushions, cigarette ends, the ears and tails of rabbits, and the dust out of the vacuum cleaner. On the other hand, it is better to avoid putting old razor-blades, broken glass, tins and nylon stockings. Mr. Easey, as you see, has a sense of humour, but I would not like to imply that this is not a deeply serious book on an important subject.

January 27, 1957

This is the time when we start ordering seeds of annuals, so I thought I would write three articles about annuals suitable for various places in the garden. Annuals for shady places, annuals for sunny places, annuals for the rock garden. *

* The other two articles will be found on pp. 30-1 and pp. 32-3.

Somehow we associate annuals with a sunny border; for the most part brightly coloured, and, by their very nature as ephemeral as the butterfly, seeming to demand all the light and gaiety they can enjoy during their brief existence. Yet there may be occasions when it becomes necessary to fill a gap with something temporary, and that gap may well occur in a shady place, let us say where plants of primrose or polyanthus have begun to die out owing to the exhaustion of some element in the soil. There is a definite soil condition known as primula sickness; all gardeners are aware that plants of this family require a constant change of ground if they are to thrive, though not everybody may be conversant with the chemical reason. Perhaps the simplest way of putting it is to say that no farmer grows the same crop on the same ground for several years in succession.

Let us assume, therefore, that we have a shady strip to fill with something for just one summer. Tobacco instantly suggests itself, *Nicotiana affinis*, and so does the night-scented stock, *Matthiola bicornis*, neither of them showy but coming into their own at dusk. There is no need, however, to condemn the shady strip to dingy colouring. *Nemophila* will show its blue, and *Anchusa capensis* its even brighter blue. *Cynoglossum amabile*, sometimes listed as *Omphalodes linifolia*, approaches perhaps nearest of all to a real gentian blue. *Impatiens balsamina*, the balsam, comes in a variety of colours, pink, red, yellow, white, sometimes spotted, and is well named Touch-me-not, for its seeds scatter at a touch and reappear as seedlings whether you want them or not. The mimulus or Monkey-flower gives a dash of orange, yellow, and flame; if the shady border is also moist, so much the better. None of these could be reproached with drabness.

There are also biennials, if you are thinking of a shady place for more than one summer. Foxgloves can be had in many a desirable strain; *Lunaria*, the old honesty of cottage

gardens, is useful with its mauvish-pink flowers followed
by the silver coins of its seed-pods in autumn; forget-me-
not is quite happy in shade; the yellow evening primrose,
Oenothera biennis, looks tall and handsome at the back; and,
if you possess a peaty soil or can make up a peaty bed, what
could be more rewarding than the blue Himalayan poppy,
Meconopsis betonicifolia?

January 29, 1956

When the early settlers first found themselves self-exiled
in that wild and dangerous territory of North America now
known to their descendants as Virginia, they discovered in
the thickets and undergrowth a shrubby thing that reminded them of the common old hazel they had known in
England. They took the forked twigs and used them for
dowsing or water-divining, as they had used hazel-twigs at
home. This was *Hamamelis virginiana*, and they called it
the witch-hazel, because any twig that would twitch in the
hand must necessarily have something to do with a witch
or a wizard. A pleasing derivation, but our own hazel has
no botanical connection with *hamamelis*, and much as we
may appreciate its catkins in spring and the squirrels its
nuts in autumn, we must not allow ourselves to be misled.

The witch-hazels we now grow in our gardens are far
better than the one our forefathers found in Virginia.
Hamamelis virginiana is a very poor thing compared with
the Chinese *Hamamelis mollis* or the Japanese *Hamamelis
arborea*. These have both been coming into their full beauty
since Twelfth Night. They are queer-looking plants, with
their twisted growth and their twisted ribbons of flower.
One always regrets not having planted more of a thing one
likes. This may not be good English, but it is good gardening
advice. If I could go back twenty years, I should plant a
whole little grove of the two Asiatics, and should now have
many large bushes to chop from, instead of being stingy

about the few twigs I spare to give my friends. The witch-hazel does not lend itself happily to cutting, which is a pity, for it is ideal as a picked flower, very long-lasting, decorative and capable of scenting a whole room. But it never seems to break out again, as most flowering shrubs do, so when you cut you spoil the chance of next year's shoot. This is the sort of warning that books never give. One has to find out for oneself.

Apart from this drawback, there could be no more accommodating shrub. It may be rather slow of development, but it will start to flower quite young, and will accept any reasonable soil, preferably of a loamy nature. It likes sunlight, to ripen its wood, but will stand up to cold winds even from the north and east, and its flowers are extraordinarily frost-resistant. On winter mornings you can see the crinkled gold coming through the rime like sugared crystallized fruits. If I add to this that in the autumn the leaves turn as yellow as a quince, perhaps I shall have said enough to encourage a wider use of this strangely neglected treasure.

February

ANNUALS for sunny places are for the most part so well known and so widely grown that it would be almost an insult to list them, and a waste of space to remind you of such things as clarkia, alyssum, candytuft, eschscholtzia, petunia, or even nemesia which certainly gives the highest value for brilliance of colour. Any seedsman's catalogue will gladly propel your memory in the direction of the obvious.

It might therefore be more useful if I were to single out a few which, although quite as easy to grow, seem to have remained oddly bashful with a dislike of publicity. I never tire of recommending *Phacelia campanularia*, and never cease to be surprised when visitors to my garden ask me what it is. Try it. Sow it at intervals of a fortnight from April onwards; put down slug-bait; thin it out to 6 in. apart; and then see what you think of it. Sheets of blue. Then there are the South Africans: *Venidium, Ursinia, Dimorphoteca*, all in the range of yellow to orange; and if you want to increase the orange touch on the palette of your border, there is *Cosmea Orange Ruffles*, 3 ft. tall, feathery of leaf, starry of flower, long-lasting, and pretty enough in a mixed bunch to please even Mrs. Constance Spry. At the foot of all these yellow-to-orange things, you might sow a vast patch of *Limmanthes douglasii*, beloved of bees, and more descriptively known as the poached-egg flower. I should not have called it poached egg myself: I should have

called it scrambled egg with chopped parsley; poached
suggests something far more circular and cohesive. I know
this is a very ordinary annual to recommend, but one does
so easily forget old favourites that a reminder may be
forgiven.

Looking back on what I have just written, I see I said
sow a vast patch. I am sure this is good and sound advice.
Always exaggerate rather than stint. Masses are more
effective than mingies.

To conclude. Have you grown *Molucella lævis?* It was
introduced into this country from Syria in 1570, nearly
400 years ago, and seems to have been somewhat neglected
until a recent revival of its popularity. I tried it and was
disappointed when it first came up; then, as it developed,
I saw that it did deserve its other name, the Shell-flower,
and from being disappointed I came round to an affection for
it. One must be patient with it, for it takes some leisurely
summer weeks before it shows what it intends to do.

I was given to understand that it could be picked and kept
in a vase indoors throughout the winter, but alas the ruthless hoe came along before I had time to arrest it, and my
Shell-flower got carted off on to the rubbish heap.

February 5, 1956

When my sons were very much younger than they now
are, they used sometimes to reproach me by saying, 'If you
haven't done that yet, you ought to of.' This magnificently
ungrammatical reproof has lingered in my mind for the
last thirty years. It still stings me. If I haven't done that
yet, I ought to of.

I ought to have ordered seeds for sowing. Catalogues
pour in, and the wealth offered is most confusing. We lose
our way amongst many temptations. Shall we order seeds
of perennials which will take two seasons before they give
any rich return? Shall we order annuals which will give

their bright brief show this summer to come? Maybe it is
best to stick to annuals in this article, but there is one
outstanding perennial which is perhaps best treated as an
annual. If it is sown under glass now, it should flower from
July to October. This is the Pacific strain of delphinium.
It includes blues such as *Blue Jay* and *Summer Skies*; purple
such as *King Arthur*; whites such as *Galahad* and *Percival*.
It is a superb strain, which can also be sown out of doors
in March or April.

Most people are faithful to the usual annuals of their
choice, but a few suggestions may not come amiss. There
is a fairly new sweet pea, growing in a tight little round
clump about a foot high, smothered in flower; this should
be a useful fill-up for odd spaces in the front of a border. It
has a sentimental name, *Little Sweetheart*. Then there is
Cleome Pink Queen, the Spider plant; it does not really look
like a spider, so spider-dislikers need not hesitate to grow it.
Three foot tall, it is useful for a gap in the middle border.
Then let me suggest the Red Mountain Orach, *Atriplex
hortensis*, a morose mahogany coloured spinach; no flower,
but richly decorative as a dark foil of foliage; and you can
eat it in salads.

If you want something more showy, especially in the
bright blues, do not omit *Cynoglossum amabile*. This served
me so well last summer that I should like to sow ounces and
ounces of it all over the place, letting it come up in any odd
corner like the wind where it listeth. And that gentian blue
annual I never tire of recommending, *Phacelia campanularia*. I implore you to sow it at fortnightly intervals from
April to June, when it will give you a succession all through
the summer. How bright and gay these annuals are. What
a pity that their life should be so brief, but perhaps that is
their charm: soon come, soon gone, a flash of beauty, then
death for them, but a renewal of life for us who can sow
their seeds and bring them to life again.

February 10, 1957

Annuals for rock-gardens? This is surely a suggestion calculated to horrify anyone who regards a rock-garden as a sanctuary for alpine plants expertly set in specially composed pockets between rock and rock, according to their demands of sun or shade, north or south aspect, scree or peat, moisture or drainage. I respect these purists, and should like nothing better than to emulate them. One must, however, consider the case of the humbler amateur, whose ledges and crevices might look sadly bare without the help of those useful little packages of seed.

I would make a condition that any annuals thus admitted should be suitable in scale and in character. The point is perhaps not worth emphasizing, for it would be a duffer of a gardener who introduced heavy solid flowers such as snapdragons amongst the small delicacies of his alpines. The maximum height should not exceed the few inches of *Phacelia*, for example, with a comparably light habit of growth. *Leptosiphon*, now called *Gilia hybridus*, is as feathery as asparagus fern and as parti-coloured as confetti. The tiny *Trachelium*, a mist of blue, although strictly speaking a perennial, is best grown as an annual because it is not quite hardy. The inch-high forget-me-not, *Myosotis alpestris*, and the alpine poppy, *Papaver alpinum*, 2 or 3 in., although not true annuals, may be treated as such, for they will flower the first season even if they do not survive many winters. *Linaria flava*, or *Antirrhinum pumilum*, is a true annual from the Mediterranean, very graceful and pretty, especially if allowed enough space to expand into a little bushlet. Smallest of all, with the longest name, is *Ionopsidium acaule* from Portugal, the Violet cress or diamond flower, which sows itself freely in tufts in odd corners and between the cracks of paving. Anything but ostentatious, it provides a miniature surprise for peering eyes. Wee, cowering and timorous, it prefers to hide itself within the veil of slight shade.

In contrast, the *Portulaca*, rightly called the Sun-plant, may be grown as a carpeter in the driest, grittiest pocket available, and so may *Mesembryanthemum criniflorum*, the Livingstone daisy. Both of these astonish with the harlequin of their colouring. They creep, crawl and kindle whenever the sun coaxes them open. With twilight they fold themselves up for the night, nor will they make much of a showing on a cloudy day. In spite of this drawback I would not be without them, for the proportion of sunny hours in our summer is perhaps greater than our national grumpiness would like us to believe.

February 12, 1956

That frail and lovely little gladiolus *colvillei The Bride* should have been potted up before Christmas, but it is not too late to do so now. If I had a stony, sun-baked terrace on the Riviera I should grow it by the hundred; as it is, I content myself with a dozen in two pots under glass. I know very well that people do grow it out of doors in England, lifting the corms each autumn as you would do with other gladioli, but its white delicacy is really seen to better advantage as a picked flower than lost in the competition of the garden.

Some gardeners have a theory that the corms are not worth keeping after the first year and that it is better to renew annually. I believe this to be an unnecessarily extravagant idea. The little offsets always to be found clustering round the parent corm may be grown on until they come to flowering size in their second year. Naturally, this means a preliminary gap of one season, but once the rhythm is established the succession is assured. I have found that the same system works with *Acidenthera bicolor Murielae*, itself a form of gladiolus, and with those tiny starry narcissi *Watereri*, which are difficult to keep otherwise and rather expensive to buy. These, by the way, are a real treasure for a pan in an Alpine house, or in a raised trough out of doors where they can be examined at leisure and more or less at eye-level.

An easier treasure on a staging under glass is the winter aconite. I somewhat nervously lifted a few clumps from the garden just as they were beginning to hump themselves in their round-shouldered way through the ground before the snow came, and transferred them with a fat ball of soil into a couple of low pans. They do not seem to have minded in the least, and are flowering like little suns, a gay sight on a winter morning. It is remarkable how frost-resistant their soft petals are. There is no heating in that greenhouse, and the pans are frozen solid, yet the golden petals remain untouched and I know that when the snow has cleared away, their garden companions will flaunt regardless of how many degrees may follow after the disappearance of the warm white blanket.

Meanwhile a Christmas present has been causing us some amusement. This is a thermometer which registers both the indoor and the outdoor temperature. You attach it to the wall of the living-room and poke a little metal gadget through the window-frame to dangle outside. It really works. You can sit snug and watch the mercury on one half of the clock-face rising from 60 degrees to 65 degrees, and on the other descending from 30 degrees to 20 degrees. Apart from this innocent fun, it has a practical application in giving a warning that some particular tender plant had better be hurriedly covered up for the night.

It came from Max Mezger Ltd., Grafton House, 2 and 3 Golden Square, London, W.1, and it is called the Monotherm.

February 17, 1957

Writing about annuals to fill gaps in the rock-garden reminded me that many rockery owners might wish to propagate their own true alpines for themselves, or to add variety to their collections by means of seed-sowing.

There are three main methods of propagation: by division, by cuttings, and by seed. Division is best carried out in the spring, when it will be found that a good plant, on being dug up and carefully pulled to pieces, will probably make four or six of itself; replant them all very firmly, do not let them lack water before they have had time to form a new root-system, and do not let a strong sun scorch them either. An inverted flower-pot is a simple safeguard.

Cuttings are rather more complicated, even if you are familiar with the general principles, chiefly because the cuttings of most alpines are so tiny to handle. Who has not gazed in admiration at the neat rows inserted into sand in a nurseryman's propagating frame, and reflected that the operation must demand the precision of a jeweller's fingers? Still, if you have the courage to try, get an old wooden box, knock out the bottom, and stand the frame on a bed of very coarse ash or clinkers. Cover this drainage foundation with an inch or two of finer ash, and then fill the frame to a depth of 3 or 4 in. with fine, sharp sand; not builders' sand, but what nurserymen call silver sand or washed river-sand. Flatten this down as tight and level as possible; get a pane of glass the right size to set over the top of the box, and your home-made frame is ready for use.

Oddments to remember.—There should be a good air-space between the glass and the cuttings. Keep the under-side of the glass free from condensation every day, if not twice a day, otherwise it will drip on to the cuttings and probably rot them. Turning the glass over is quicker than wiping it. Always press your cuttings very firmly into their bed of sand: a cutting which will come out at the twitch of finger and thumb is not a well-set cutting, as many an unlicked young postulant gardener has found to his sorrow when the old boss came by. You might try Vermiculite as a substitute for sand as a rooting medium, and also remember that hormone preparations make the rooting of cuttings much easier. Seradix A or B is a great help, and can be bought from any nurseryman in a bottle bringing its own instructions with it. It can also be bought from some chemists, but I suppose that if I were to mention the admirable horticultural department of Messrs. Boots the editorial pencil in *The Observer* office would cross it out as a 'free advertisement.'

Carried away by enthusiasm for cuttings and how to take them, I have left myself no space for remarks about growing alpines from seed. (See February 24, 1957.)

February 19, 1956

I am not at all sure that I approve of tabloid gardening. I like to think of old gardeners pottering their life-time away in green baize aprons, straw hats, a twist of raffia behind their ears, and a Nannie-like intimacy with the plants under their care. Nowadays people prefer things to be made easy for them, perhaps because modern life is too busy and intricate for specialization, and so we get book societies telling us what we ought to read, and nurserymen's catalogues telling us what we ought to plant.

It does save trouble, and I suppose must be tolerated as a symptom. For the bewildered novice it is certainly convenient to be offered what are described as Collections: they range from the Best Border Perennials to the Best Plants for Crazy Paving. You will note that they are usually called The Best. This does not necessarily mean the most choice, but it does generally mean the most reliable. I quote from one catalogue, proposing a Rock Garden Collection: 'All are good hearty growers with no special fads or fancies . . . free flowering and of bright showy colours . . . selected, so far as is possible, to give a succession of flower from Spring to Autumn. We feel confident that this Collection will give

pleasure to those who want an effective display without a
lot of fuss and trouble.' No doubt it will and, moreover, you
know exactly what you are going to spend, from thirty-six
plants at £3 7s. 6d. to 180 plants at £13 10s. 0d.*

I don't like it; it goes against every grain of my make-up;
what I enjoy doing is to make a success of something rather
difficult to manage; yet why should I try to impose my own
quirks on the readers of these articles? The beginner must
be considered as well as the connoisseur. Gardening is ter-
ribly confusing at the start (and even at the end, believe
me). There seem to be such myriads of plants, all equally
desirable, all so tempting to order, all setting out with such
promise as one unwraps them from their strawy bundles or
unpacks them from their little pots, all so heart-breakingly
liable to disappear before they have completed one year of
life. Infant mortality in the Middle Ages is the only
approximate comparison.

It is to the beginner who wants a short-cut to his objective
that I commend a study of the Collections listed in these
kindly caressive catalogues.

February 24, 1957

Alpines from seed. This is a real enterprise for the
amateur enthusiast. It may require patience. Many alpines
do not germinate within a few weeks of sowing, even if the
seeds are sown as soon as they ripen. You may have to wait
for twelve months before those heartening little green
growths suddenly begin to appear in your pans or seed-
boxes. I suppose it is now a well-known dodge to leave the
pans or boxes out of doors, to let them get frozen hard and
covered by snow, and then to bring them into a warm place
when they will, as gardeners say, jump to it. Being frozen
hard is the sort of treatment that most alpines expect and

* This was the Spring catalogue of Messrs. Wallace & Barr, the Old
Gardens, Tunbridge Wells.

understand; I shouldn't like it myself, but they seem to. You could even put your pans or boxes into the refrigerator if you could find room between the herrings and the butter, and then bring them into the warmth of a room or a cool greenhouse to start them into germination.

Many alpine plants may easily be raised from seed. Roughly speaking, they need a gritty compost and rather careful watering when they start to come up, and a careful pricking-out as they begin to attain pricking-out size, but then that might be said of any specially choice and chosen plant that one has elected to raise from its beginning in those extraordinary little grains, as small and dusty as a pinch of pepper or snuff. Otherwise, they are no more difficult than anything else, and if you have some experience of seed-sowing you will find this a most repaying method of increasing your stock of alpines at little cost. I do find, however, that not everybody knows where to find a wider selection of seeds than those advertised by most of the big commercial growers. This seems to me very odd, for there is a certain firm which celebrated its centenary two years ago, and whose seed list now runs to over 4,000 numbers. There is practically nothing you can't get from them. Of course I mean Messrs. Thompson and Morgan, Ipswich.

February 26, 1956

I refer you to p. 37 for an article I provided for the puzzled novice willing to avail himself of the convenient Collections lists supplied in the catalogues of some nurserymen; I now rush to the opposite extreme with a note on a family of plants calculated to challenge the skill of the most advanced gardener. I mean the terrestrial orchids.

As we know, our native orchids are in grave danger of extermination for one reason or another. Not the least of these dangers is the well-meaning effort of the amateur who, armed with a trowel, imagines that he can dig them up and transport them to safety in his own plot of ground. He is excited at having come on a stray specimen on the chalk downs or in moist woodland. Some vandal, he argues, will come along and destroy the treasure, so he had better rescue it himself while there is yet time. He has a vision of picnickers, gathering recklessly, unaware of the old rhyme,

> Orchis cut is Orchis still,
> But Orchis plucked is Orchis nil,

meaning that if you tug the flower-stalk from its base you may irretrievably damage the tuberous root-stock. So off he goes with his prize in a trug, replants it carefully, and feels aggrieved when it fails to reappear.

It was thus with pleasure that I received a long list of the hardy terrestrial orchids, with the guarantee that none of these plants had been robbed from Great Britain. No devastation of our own sparse supply. The orchids offered in this list have been collected from all over Europe, and some of them might do well with skilful handling. The Marsh orchids (Dactylorchises), though by no means the most beautiful, are perhaps the least unmanageable. They seem also to be extremely long-suffering. I remember a curious instance of their fortitude and forbearance. There was a lawn, regularly mown for at least half a century, pure virtuous turf with never a weed or a stranger in it. War came, and stopped lawn-mowing as it stopped several other equally genial pursuits. The grass grew, turning that smooth lawn into a meadow sprinkled all over with the green-veined hooded *Orchis morio*. Where had it been hiding, all that time, its hopeful shoots shaved off year after year by the remorseless blades of the mower? How did the tuber contrive to exist, denied the natural fulfilment of its foliage?

This little anecdote should at least have an encouraging effect on those bold spirits who would like to secure the list I referred to. It includes prices and cultural directions, and may be obtained from G. B. Rawinsky, 384 Whitton Avenue East, Greenford, Middlesex.

March

March 3, 1957

I AM often asked about camomile lawns, by people under the mistaken impression that I have got one myself. I did attempt some very unsuccessful little paths, however, which have sufficed to show me that camomile hates a shady situation, overhanging trees, and a stodgy soil. The only lawn I have ever seen is in full sun (in the heart of London) and fully lives up to its reputation as a hard-wearing ground cover, harder-wearing than turf, for it gets trampled on by thousands of feet and never seems to show any ill effects. I believe also that it requires mowing less frequently than grass, a great advantage in days when one has to think of avoiding labour.

One sows the seed in drills on a prepared bed; thins out; and transplants the little tufts in due course to the place where they are wanted. They spread fairly rapidly, and the more you squash them flat to the ground the better. The first cutting might have to be done with shears, or at any rate with the blades of a machine set high, because before it has had time to grow into a sward camomile comes up into wiry stalks and might easily get tugged out altogether. This wiriness disappears after a time, leaving a close plat which by the unobservant would probably be mistaken for an unusually dark green turf. I do not say that camomile has quite the beauty of mown grass, so smooth and fine, green-gold in the sunlight, olive in the long shadows; but for practical purposes it should serve you well.

It goes without saying that the necessary cutting will deprive you of the flowers. They are ugly little things, not to be regretted, unless indeed you wish to make camomile tea or to wash your hair in a decoction or to make an antiseptic lotion which you can do by mixing the flowers with dragon's blood, old swallows' nests, worm-eaten oak, and the fat of a mountain mouse.

March 4, 1956

I was surprised and pleased to come upon an old friend in a florist's shop. Frankly, it was so long since I had seen it that I had forgotten all about it, and then discovered that it is much less widely grown than it used to be. There seems to be no particular reason for this, since it demands only a temperate greenhouse, is by no means difficult, and is certainly most desirable as a pot-plant. (It does not pick well.) The thing I mean is called *Bouvardia*.

At first sight, you might take it for a tightly compressed bunch of a white jasmine which had been subjected to that iniquitous fashion of dyeing flowers an unnatural colour by standing them in water diluted with the requisite tint of ink. It shares the tubular shape of a jasmine, growing in a corymb or cluster, each individual flower flattening out at the tip to the circular size of a farthing. More fleshy than a jasmine, it looks as though it ought to be as strongly scented as a gardenia or a stephanotis; one's first impulse is to bury one's nose, only to meet with disappointment; the waxy appearance is most misleading; the thing has no scent at all.

Colour it has, and that is the point of it. How to describe colour in words? If I say cyclamen-pink, or cherry-pink, or Rose du Barry, or Persian red, I may be conveying quite the wrong impression to another person. All I can say is that those bunches of *Bouvardia* were warming to the heart and eye in contrast with the snow outside. They looked as genial as gleed or embers on a hearth-fire.

As a matter of fact, there are three *Bouvardias* said to be
scented: *B. humboldtii*, *B. jasminiflora*, and *B. longiflora*.
These are all white. Must we be driven to the conclusion
that we cannot exact both scent and colour? Would that be
asking too much? For my own part, I think I would forgo
the scent in favour of the crammed bunches so softly pink,
so deeply roseate, of *B. angustifolia* or *B. triphylla*.

Their native home is Mexico, and the R.H.S. big
Dictionary of Gardening gives their date of introduction
into England as 1857. With all respect, I think this must
be erroneous, as I find *Bouvardia* mentioned in a copy of
Loudoun's *Encyclopædia of Gardening*, dated 1822. However this may be, it is extremely difficult to procure plants
today. I know where to get seeds of *B. triphylla*, but have
so far failed to trace any source of a more varied supply
from Messrs. Thompson and Morgan, Ipswich. If any
correspondent could advise me, I should be so grateful.

March 10, 1957

When writing about propagation I sometimes wonder
how many readers find my suggestions intelligible. I
imagine that even a schoolchild knows the principles of
seed-sowing, but perhaps the instruction to 'take cuttings
in the usual way' is not very helpful to those who do not
know what the usual way is.

Roughly speaking, there are two kinds of plant which
lend themselves to increase by cuttings: the hard-wooded
and the soft-wooded. The hard-wooded are the flowering
and the evergreen shrubs, such as Forsythia and sweet-bay;
roses; and fruit bushes. To take the cuttings, which is best
done in September or October, you choose young shoots
which have ripened during the summer, and either pull
them away from the parent stem with a heel, or cut them
off close below one of their own nodes or joints. Anything
up to 15 in. is a good length. Take off the lower leaves and

the soft unripened tips, set your cuttings upright in a sandy trench which you will previously have prepared with a spade, press them very firmly into the sand, fill in the trench, stamp the soil down, and leave it until the cuttings have formed their roots, when they can safely be transplanted.

This outdoor method is the simplest, as all you need worry about afterwards is to see that frost has not heaved up the cuttings and loosened them. If you want to be on the safer side, however, you can follow the same procedure in a closed frame, but then you will have to worry about moisture and also about ventilation.

There are a few shrubs which will not root from cuttings, such as magnolias, azaleas, some rhododendrons, camellias, choisyas, some daphnes—all these have to be layered.

Soft-wooded plants which may be increased by cuttings include herbaceous things such as lupins, delphiniums, phlox, which in the spring provide many young shoots from the root. These are best set in pots of sandy compost, and kept in a frame until rooted.

This is all very elementary and incomplete, but if anybody wants more information, illustrated by many practical photographs, there is a useful book called *Pictorial Plant Propagation*, by G. F. Gardiner, published by C. Arthur Pearson, Ltd., at 18s. It deals not only with cuttings, but with seed-sowing, layering, grafting, and several up-to-date methods involving the use of polythene.

March 11, 1956

Some people like daisies in their turf; others don't. Jean-Jacques Rousseau ascribed pinky eyelashes to it, thought it a general favourite, and called it the *robin* of flowers. To John Skelton it was 'daisie delectable.' Beaumont and Fletcher thought it 'smell-less, yet most quaint,' incorrectly, for a bunch of daisies has a peculiarly earthy smell, especially when it comes as a hot little gift in the hand of a child. Wordsworth, peering closely, noticed that it cast a shadow to 'protect the lingering dewdrop from the sun.' Tennyson, who was usually extremely accurate about such matters, went very wrong when he claimed for Maud that

> . . . her feet have touched the meadows
> And left the daisies rosy,

for this is simply not true. Enchanted by this idea, I wasted many youthful summer hours stamping on daisies, in fact I still do, but never a daisy has so far blushed beneath my tread.

Fortunately for those who like their turf green and not speckled, it is very easy for them to reverse the old song and give their answer to Daisy. A selective weed-killer will do the trick economically and with a great saving of labour, though it may be necessary to go twice with the lethal watering-can over the ground. Good turf certainly looks better just after it has been mown, without those flattened patches, though there is perhaps something to be said for the small 'companion of the sun' when it has reappeared within a day or two.

The cultivated varieties of *Bellis perennis* come under quite a different heading. These will be grown in soil, not in grass, and are most evocative of old kitchen gardens where they were so often used as an edging to paths. The cottage *Hen-and-Chickens* should never be forgotten; it consorts well with the double primroses, for anyone who can persuade these charming but fickle creatures to thrive. *Rob Roy*, a deep red, is somewhat smaller and less domestically minded; *Alice*, with a Victorian suggestion in her name, is suitably pink and quilled. A tiny, best suited to a trough or the rock-garden, is the bright pink *Dresden China*, truly as pretty as porcelain, the perfect companion both in scale and character to our native forget-me-not, *Myosotis alpestris*.

These daisies are all hardy, but are best renovated from time to time by pulling the clumps to pieces and replanting firmly. I wonder whether the old gardeners ever troubled to do this? Plants seem to exact far more attention nowadays. They seem to be aware that they live in a Welfare State and to resent being left to take care of themselves.

March 17, 1957

May it be forgiven if for once an 'In Your Garden' article makes no attempt to be of any practical use in your garden at all? I am on the Equator as I write these notes, half-way across the world, and, not being a blasé traveller, am far too preoccupied with the odd things I have seen and odd facts I have learnt, to think soberly of the duties which confront the gardener in an English spring.

Amongst the odd though perhaps not very useful bits of information I have picked up, I never knew that coffee, like the pigeon orchid, flowered after a sudden drop in temperature, in the case of the orchid exactly and invariably nine days; I did not know that more tapioca was used in the manufacture of glue and glossy paper for illustrated magazines than for all the milk puddings in the world's nurseries, nor that kapok came from the forest tree with a hollow trunk that echoes like a drum, nor that the frangipani tree was planted in cemeteries for the scented blooms, in falling, to carpet the graves, nor that monkeys could be be trained to collect rare orchids from the tops of trees, nor that the Malayans used coral instead of stone in their rockgardens. I had never realized that annuals, given tropical conditions, would produce seeds within three months of sowing and, since they flower continuously in countries where winter is unknown, would supply four generations in one year. Nor had I ever been sufficiently grateful for not living in an island where the nocturnal burglar blows the pollen of *Datura* in though your open window by means of a blowpipe, and helps himself to your possessions while you lie temporarily insensible.

Of the beauty of some flowering trees it would be tantalizing to speak, for many of them cannot be induced to flower for us, even given the appropriate warmth and humidity of a greenhouse. This, apparently, is due to the extreme importance of long hours of daylight. Whether the difficulty could be overcome by artificial rays remains to be seen. There are reports that it is being tried in America.

March 18, 1956

The first flowers to appear are very small. One wonders why this should be. Is it because some curious provision of Nature teaches them to crouch low to the ground, less exposed to the blasts and gales they may expect, even as the high alpines flatten themselves in cushions against the boulders in the turf of the windy pastures? Think how small they are, the first things we hope to see: the snowdrops, the snow-flakes, the aconites, the scillas, the chionodoxas, the grape-hyacinths, cyclamen coum, the dwarf irises *reticulata* and *histrioïdes*, the miniature narcissi *bulbocodium*, *cyclamineus*, *triandrus* and *juncifolius*. It is perhaps understandable that they should be small; but how ingenious of them to be so flexible, bending instead of breaking under the rough breath of a gale or beneath the weight of snow.

These reflections led me to the consideration of a, to my mind, important question of taste in gardening. It is the question of the scale and proportion of plants grown, in relation to the size of the garden. It is rather difficult to explain what I mean, in so short an article, but let me put it like this; enormous trumpet daffodils such as *Golden Harvest* overweight a little grassy orchard of perhaps two dozen young apple-trees, whereas a planting of *Narcissus bulbocodium* or even of our native *Lent Lily*, would be more suitable and congruous. The same idea can be extended to the flowering shrubs. Rhododendrons are handsome, but are they not better suited to vast areas than to the normal stretch of garden we can cope with today? Surely it is preferable to choose the lighter, more delicate-looking things, for a limited space, than the huge heavy things better adapted to the grand gardens of the past?

We have come down to a modest measure, and must accommodate ourselves accordingly. We shall not lose much, in fact we shall gain, if we realize that we can and should plant in accordance with the space we have at our disposal.

We should not think of putting a water-colour into a big black frame. We should not think of putting an oil-painting into a cardboard-mount. I think the same principle should apply in gardening.

March 24, 1957

It is said that some 3,000 years ago Queen Hatshepset sent a fleet to fetch incense-bearing trees from the Land of Punt. These trees, of which thirty-one were successfully transplanted to the temple at Luxor, belonged to the genus *Boswellia*, which produces the resin we still know and use and call frankincense.

These reflections have been induced in me by the fact that I write these words sailing along on precisely the same latitude as the Land of Punt. The story goes to prove that the plant-collecting instinct, or desire to add to the indigenous vegetation of one's own country, is of very ancient origin in man. Sometimes, as in the case of Queen Hatshepset, it has been deliberate and undertaken at considerable expense; sometimes it has been accidental or incidental on some other enterprise, as befell Sir Stamford Raffles when, travelling in the wild mountains of Sumatra in 1818, he had the alarming experience of coming on the hitherto unknown and by far the largest flower in the world. Purple and brick-red in colour, it measured over a yard across, contained a gallon and a half of water, and weighed fifteen pounds. Not without good reason, it received the name *Rafflesia* in his honour. Sometimes, again, one country has acquired the flowers of another through a disaster due to natural causes. Thus some bulbs of *Vallota speciosa*, intended for Holland, were cast up on the coast of Yorkshire in or about 1790 with the wreck of a Dutch ship trying to make her way home from the little colony at the foot of Table Mountain. The canny Yorkshiremen picked them up, since when Vallota has always been familiarly known as the Scarborough Lily. *Nerine sarniensis* also, and for the same reason, got itself distributed into northern waters a good way short of its intended destination, for in 1659 it was washed up unnoticed on Guernsey, where to everybody's astonishment it flowered in its natural season a few months later. It was thought to have come from Japan, since the ship had sailed from the Far East; only later was it found growing wild in Cape Province; but it made no difference, for it has always been called the Guernsey Lily.

March 25, 1956

The time has come to plant out bulbs which have flowered in bowls in the house. If this is done regularly every year, it is surprising to see what a collection accumulates in a very short space of time, and how quickly they settle down to their new conditions. It may be true that a strongly forced bulb will not flower again, out of doors, until the second season; but as most of us start our bowls in a cool, dark cupboard and bring them into nothing more intense than the warmth of an ordinary living-room, which, in this country, is not saying much, the majority will reappear complete with bud twelve months hence.

It is no good whatsoever trying to preserve the early Roman hyacinths or the paper-white narcissus, but all other hyacinths and all other narcissi (daffodils) lend themselves very obligingly to our wishes. Hyacinths should be planted shallow, with the nose of the bulb only just below soil-level. Narcissus wants to go deeper; and if you are planting in grass, as is the common practice, it is easy to cut three sides of a square of turf, hinge it back, set your bulbs in the hole, hinge the turf into place again, and stamp upon it with all the weight of Miss Jekyll's Boots. (*See frontispiece.*)

I treat my bowl-grown bulbs pretty rough. They must take their chance, as I must take mine. They have done their best for me, once, and if only they will repeat even a second-best effort I shall be grateful. The most I do for them is to cut off their spent flowers to save them the effort of seeding, and make them a present of their green leaves necessary to the development of the bulb underground. These leaves look untidy for a bit, I know; they flop in a miserable dejective yellowing sheaf; the only thing to do with them if you want to keep them neat is to tie them into a knot of themselves. On no account cut them off.

You probably know all this already, so may I add two little reminders? It is so easy to forget these seasonal jobs, and then the moment has passed and it is too late. The first is to remember that this is the time to lift snowdrops, if you want to concentrate them instead of letting them remain scattered in odd clumps. Snowdrops do not mind being dug up while their leaf is still green; in fact, for some reason which I do not attempt to explain, it is the only way they enjoy removal. My second reminder applies to that brave little crocus, *Tomasinianus*, which comes up in a mauve mist in February, and is now setting its seed. Save that seed. Throw it down, broadcast, even into grass; wait four years; and then see the result.

March 31, 1957

Arriving home after two months' absence abroad, what did I find of interest awaiting me in an accumulation of correspondence? I think I had better compose this article somewhat scrappily from a few chosen bits.

The most exciting news was that the climbing strawberry is now available in this country. Readers of my gardening notes may perhaps remember that last year (July 22, 1956) I wrote about this strange new plant which grew 6 to 7 ft. high and could be trained up a post or against a trellis, but which was so jealously guarded by its raisers on the Continent that all export was forbidden. If you bought a plant in Switzerland, Germany, or France you had to give your word of honour that you would not bring it away. But now we are allowed it. It is expensive, at 10s. 6d. each or 50s. for five, and five is the most that can be supplied to any customer; so you should order at once from the only distributor, Messrs. Baker, Codsall, Wolverhampton.

This climbing strawberry, called Sonjana, is certainly a thing that every enterprising gardener should attempt. Its advantages are obvious: no strawing, no splashing from mud after rain, no crawling slugs, no stooping to gather the fruit. Besides, it looks very pretty, and claims to crop from June to October.*

The next outstanding item in my correspondence concerned the difficulty of raising daphnes from cuttings. I had written an article (March 10, 1957) saying that, amongst other shrubs such as rhododendrons, etc., daphnes did not take kindly to this method of propagation. Indignant letters informed me of great successes; but, I noticed, they invariably referred to *Daphne odora*. Never a mention of *D.*

* Since writing the above the climbing strawberry has had the test of one summer. Messrs. Baker have printed a leaflet of advice. They emphasize the need for good feeding, and report that some customers complained the plant did not grow tall enough: this they attribute to an early drought.

mezereum or *retusa* or *tangutica* or *collina*; least of all to that rare and lovely Chinese *D. genkwa*, which is notoriously resistant to all the normal methods of increase. It looks therefore as though *D. odora* and its variety *Odora variegata* are amenable to cuttings, whereas the others of the family are not.

I must add that one correspondent repeated a charming suggestion. He saw a plant of *D. odora* in a cottage garden, and inquired whether it was from a cutting. The owner said yes, but that cuttings could be taken on only four days in the year, August 26th to 50th. I do wonder how these folkloreish beliefs originate and survive. Sometimes there appears to be some truth in them, such as the sowing of certain seeds beneath a waxing or a waning moon.

Apropos of seed-sowing, it is perhaps not generally realized that delphiniums sown in March will give a certain amount of flower in the late summer, and also that it is not too late to take cuttings of established delphinium plants in early April. Vermiculite is recommended as the best rooting medium. Two first-rate booklets, at 2s. 6d. each, on *Delphiniums from Seed* and *How to Grow Good Delphiniums*, are obtainable from R. Parrett, Yew Cottage, Fairmile Lane, Cobham, Surrey, profusely illustrated.

April

April 1, 1956

IF anybody is thinking of making an ornamental pond, or of improving one already in existence, this is a good time of year to plan it since many water-plants like being planted in May, and what more agreeable occupation than to plan it over Easter, that hope-full patch of holiday?*

Ponds vary in size and in character. Pond is an ugly word; I prefer pool. Pool rhymes with cool, and that is what a pool ought to be, a place to sit by on a summer evening, watching the reflections in the water, and the swallows swooping after the insects on a level flight. It is not possible to lay down rules, since every pool will vary in size, shape, depth and situation, but here at least are a few suggestions.

Water-lilies immediately come to the mind; I suppose everybody knows roughly how to plant these, by setting the roots between two turves, like a sandwich; tying the turves together with strong string, or even placing them in a bit of old sacking and sinking them into a foot or so of water. There is the white one, *candida*, and there are also red ones, *Froebeli* and *fulgens*; a pink one, *liliacea*, and a yellow, *sulphurea*. Then if you do not mind covering the surface of the water, there is the water-hawthorn, *Aponogeton distachyus*, which is very pretty but should perhaps be reserved for a rather larger area than the average pool; and the water-violet, *Hottonia palustris*. Personally I think it a pity to hide the water too much, unless you are anxious to make

* Easter fell on April 1st in 1956.

cover for fish; I like to see clear water in the middle, reflecting the sky and the plants which you will have set round the edge. Of these, we have our native flowering rush, *Butomus umbellatus*, tall and rosy; *Pontederia cordata*, blue; and *Sagittaria*, the arrow-head; these three are indispensable. For a low-growing plant round the margins, the water forget-me-not, *Myosotis palustris*, makes a pale blue drift and is an easy spreader. If the pool is large enough, our own native yellow iris is not to be despised; it has the advantage of keeping close into the bank and not walking out into deeper water; but if this is considered too much of a weed, there are the fine Japanese irises, *I. kaempferi*, with flat clematis-like faces, and the more slender iris *sibirica* which will grow in any moist soil but does not enjoy being permanently water-logged. The same applies to the moisture-loving primulas, but one could go on endlessly thinking of plants for the margin; the difficulty is one of selection, for the choice is varied and wide.

April 7, 1957

I believe I have never mentioned *Billbergia* in any of these articles. I can't think why. It is a most amusing pot-plant for a cool greenhouse, or even for a room indoors, since it is so nearly hardy that it asks only to be kept free from frost. I have even seen it described as 'a common cottage window plant,' though I must admit that I have never seen it on any cottage window sill. This should be enough to recommend it in these days when so many people go in for indoor gardening.

What is it like? It is difficult to describe. If I were describing it in botanical terms I should have to say its flowers were zygomorphic, stamens inserted into the base of the perianth, and what sort of a picture would that convey? No, I would rather say that it is more like a crazy jeweller's dream than a flower, an immensely long earring in the most fantastic mixture of colours: bright pink stem and bracts, with a 4-in-long dingle-dangle of green, blue, pink, and yellow, a thing to swing from the head-dress of a Balinese dancer or from the ear-lobes of a beauty in a Persian miniature. Yet even that amateurish pictorial effort cannot make you see it. Does it help if I add that it belongs to the spiky pineapple family?

Billbergia nutans is the easiest to grow. There are other varieties, some of which sound even more alluring, such as *Billbergia zebrina*, stripy as a zebra, but *nutans* is the most reliable so far as flowering goes; in fact, it has never disappointed me, flowering with the utmost liberality every March into April. If you want to increase it, you break it up after flowering into rosettes which can then be repotted, and the old ones thrown away; or else you can repot the whole plant into a larger pot with some fresh soil, rather on the light side and well drained. Kept in this way, a single plant may produce over a score of its strange, hanging flowers. The native home of the Billbergias extends from Brazil to Mexico.

I love making experiments. They mostly turn out wrong, but I cannot resist. Thus I have ordered some seed of a rapid annual climber, apparently a close relation of our old friend the *Ipomaea*, Heavenly Blue or Morning Glory. It is called *Quamoclit pinnata*, and is described as having flowers changing in colour from pinkish-orange to rose-pink in a single day. I have learnt to mistrust these descriptions, so it was really for the sake of the thing's nickname that I ordered it: Hearts and Honey.*

April 8, 1955

It always interests and amuses me to watch people going round other people's gardens. One can separate them into

---

* This did not turn out wrong. It was very pretty indeed, little flat flowers the size of a florin.

two categories. There are the Eyes and the No-eyes. The Eyes walk slowly, peering into everything, noticing everything, reading labels, taking notes, for the Eyes usually carry a notebook with them and make, with a blunt pencil, notes which they will be unable to decipher when they get home.

No-eyes stumps blindly round. He gets just a vague impression of being in somebody else's garden; it is a very nice garden he thinks; he has paid his shilling to visit it, so he is going to stay in it as long as he can and get the fullest enjoyment out of it. But does he really get the fullest enjoyment if he doesn't know how to look? Looking at flowers, and at design and lay-out is an árt which has to be learnt if you are not born with a natural gift for it, and the more you know the greater the enjoyment you get.

It is an art which may be acquired with practice, and that is why I want to urge everybody to take advantage of the opportunity offered to visit the hundreds of private gardens now open to the public. It really is such a chance to see and learn, profit and enjoy. Under the National Gardens Scheme for England and Wales considerably more than 1,000 gardens are available; in Scotland more than 200. They range from large and famous gardens to small modest gardens, so you can take your choice. The profit goes to District Nurses, with an agreed percentage to the National Trust. Lists for England and Wales may be obtained from the Organizing Secretary, National Gardens Scheme, 57 Lower Belgrave Street, London, S.W.1; and for Scotland, from the General Organizer, Scotland's Gardens Scheme, 26 Castle Terrace, Edinburgh, 1.

There are also separate lists, county by county, and the name and address of the County Organizer is given in the general list at the beginning of each county section.

The general list will cost you 2s., postage 6d., but should you wish for something more elaborate and also more expensive, let me recommend 'Gardens of Britain,' by A. G. L. Hellyer, published by *Country Life* at 30s. Illustrated by over 200 large photographs, this volume by one of the best and most authoritative writers on gardening matters describes nearly 100 gardens in private ownership but open to the public. It makes a wonderful present either to give or to receive.

April 14, 1957

The tall almond trees are over, but their tiny relation succeeds them, and is far less commonly planted, though it is pretty as can be and takes up far less room, casts no shadow, gets in nobody's way, does not rob the soil with great roots, and is apparently unattractive to sparrows, tits, or bullfinches. It is indeed the ideal shrublet either for a rock garden or to fill a gap in a narrow border given over to other choice things. It never grows taller than 2 or 3 ft.; it smothers itself in small rosy flowers in April; it runs about underground, coming up in a miniature grove of pink and green; it never makes itself a nuisance; and the only thing you must absolutely insist on when ordering it from your nurseryman is that it should be on its own roots. He will know what you mean.

This charmer goes under two names, listed either as *Prunus tenella* or as *Amygdalus nana*, the dwarf almond, or the dwarf Russian almond, and the best variety is *Gessleriana*.

If you like the shrublets, have you ever tried *Prunus cistena nana*? About 2 ft. high, with whitish-pink blossom, it can be inspected from above as though it were a full-size plum-tree seen through the wrong end of field-glasses. Or *Spiraea arguta*, which every April looks as though it would flower itself to death but never seems to, in a mass of tiny white inflorescence on arching wires of thin black twigs. This grows somewhat taller, say 5 to 6 ft. if you let it, only I fancy that by judicious snipping with the shears it could be kept to the size and shape you want. A very pretty thing, rightly nicknamed Bridal Wreath.

The species lilacs (Syringa) are not nearly well known enough, since they also are ideal for the small garden. I know I have already mentioned the variety called *Palibiniana* in this column, but there are others. There is *microphylla var. superba*, with dusky rose-red flowers; and *Sweginzowii superba*, and *Tigerstedtii*, both of them pink and scented. I feel I ought to apologize for their horrific names but it really isn't my fault, and I did want to draw your attention to this rather neglected race of what our grandparents used to call laycock.

I would recommend Messrs. Notcutt, Woodbridge, Suffolk, as suppliers.

Visitors to the Alpine Gardens Society's Show at Vincent Square on April 2nd may have been attracted to a stall exhibiting pottery. We have so little tradition of pottery in this country, compared with Italy, Spain, or Portugal, that I went with interest to see what was being done. I went full of fear of the arty-crafty, and was most agreeably surprised. Real taste, skill, and imagination were displayed. The idea of the organizers was to get good potters to make flower-pots and bowls aesthetically acceptable and functionally useful; something which could be used in the greenhouse or in the home. The address is Primavera, 149 Sloane Street, S.W.1.

April 15, 1956

When we were small, we were constantly being adjured to have more grit. When we grazed our knees falling down on gravel paths, and naturally howled, we were instantly exhorted by an undamaged grown-up not to be such a crybaby but to show grit, a brief monosyllabic synonym for

British fortitude. We thought then, bitterly, that we had got plenty of grit to exhibit in our poor knees already.

If only somebody had given me the same advice in later years when I first embarked on gardening, how grateful I should have been. Grit, grit, lots of grit, the sharper the better. I now believe it to be one of the secrets of good gardening, whether in the potting-shed or in the rock-garden. I got an Easter present (from myself to myself) of 5 cubic yards of this deliciously crumbly stuff, so I now have a heap which I hope will last me for years. The sort to ask for is called $\frac{3}{16}$ths of an inch. Hitherto I had made do with washed silver sand, but this is better.

Mixed in with loam and leaf-mould for potting, it keeps the soil beautifully open; you can squeeze a moist fistful as hard as you like and it will not coagulate. Crocks in the bottom of the pot, an inch-deep layer of sphagnum moss, and the mixture on top, is the recipe. No plant or seedling should damp off, even if you overwater, as in our anxiety we are sometimes apt to do. Then if you want to make up any special bed, say for bulbs that enjoy good drainage, you follow the same procedure by tipping a barrow-load of the grit into the required pocket, stirring it into the soil, and topping it up with an extra scatter of the grit to be washed in by rain. This ought to suit all bulbs that like a good ripening off, such as ixias, many lilies, or the little early irises of the reticulata family, including *I. histriodes* and the green-black *I. tuberosa* whose correct name is *Hermodactylus tuberosus*. I think also that we might be enabled to grow some of that reputedly difficult race, the Regelio-cyclus and Oncocylus irises . . . but I am getting carried away by the possibilities offered by grit, and must come down with a crash on to a dear, valued, very ordinary winter-flowering thing, *Iris stylosa* (*unguicularis*). I propose to plant this into a bed of pure grit, and see what happens.

One has these good intentions. How seldom one carries

them out. There is always something else to do. A gardener should have nine times as many lives as a cat.

April 21, 1957

Easter Day. It seems odd to look back to Christmas Day, but there is a gay little butter-yellow shrub in my garden which has been flowering continuously between those two great feasts of the Church, a sort of hyphen linking the Birth and the Resurrection which is more than can be said for most shrubs, so I think it deserves a write-up, as these recommendations are colloquially called, and a tribute of gratitude for the pleasure it has given me in its persistence throughout the dreary months.

The shrub I mean is called *Coronilla glauca.*

There are several sorts of coronilla. I know I shall be told that *Coronilla emerus* is the hardier, but on the whole I should advise *glauca.* I know I shall be told that it isn't quite hardy. I know it isn't supposed to be, but all I can say is that it came through the frightening frosts of February 1956, with no protection, and if a supposedly tender shrub can survive that test, it qualifies for at least a trial in the Home Counties and the south-west, though perhaps not in the Midlands, East Anglia, or the north. I must admit also that I planted it in a narrow border under the south-facing wall of the house, where it got the maximum of shelter against cold north winds or east winds; and there it still is, flowering exuberantly away, one of the most delightful surprises and successes I ever had.

I must add another word in praise of this rarely planted shrub. It has its own sense of humour. Sometimes it gives off so strong a scent as to delude me into thinking that I caught the scent of some neighbouring wall-flowers; then I discovered that the coronilla is powerfully fragrant by day and scentless by night.

This whole question of scent in plants is one which I do

not understand, though no doubt a scientific explanation is available. The warmth of the sun and the humidity of rain and dew account for much, as we all know from observation and experience, but there must be other factors unrevealed to the ignoramus. Why, for instance, does the balsam poplar waft its scent a hundred yards distant sometimes and at other times remain so obstinately scentless and sniff-less as to be imperceptible on the closest approach? These things retain their mystery for me, and I am not sure that I want the answer. A little mystery is precious to preserve.

May I assure the gentleman who writes to me (quite often) from a Priory in Sussex that I am not the armchair, library-fireside gardener he evidently suspects, 'never having performed any single act of gardening' myself, and that for the last forty years of my life I have broken my back, my finger-nails, and sometimes my heart, in the practical pursuit of my favourite occupation?

April 22, 1956

Looking back over the nastiest weeks of our late unlamented winter, I try to remember with gratitude the things that gave me pleasure when all was grey and colourless and cold outside. I managed then to keep a few square yards on a shelf or staging in an unheated greenhouse, and those few square yards were crowded with tiny bright things from New Year's Day to Easter. Their brilliance contrasted with the snow and the leaden skies; it was like coming into an aviary of tropical birds or butterflies, yet they were all easy to grow, nothing odd or recondite, just a few pans of the early species crocus; a pot of *Cyclamen coum* which flowered so madly I thought it might kill itself by its generosity; a pan-full of grape hyacinths dug up out of the garden; some snowdrops lifted just before they intended to flower; some saxifrages sprouting into miniature nail-head-size of flower, hugging close to the tight grey-green rosettes they pinkly star; some early flowering narcissi and jonquils; a pot-plant of the lovely pink camellia *Donation*; some early primulus, *frondosa* and *marginata var. Linda Pope*; a pot of the scented daphnes *collina* and *tangutica*; and, bravest and earliest of all, the miniature sky-blue iris *histrioides major*, which I recommend to everybody, either for indoors or out. It is ideal in an Alpine pan and ideal in a sink or trough.

A sprinkling of grey granite or limestone chippings goes a long way towards enhancing the colour and delicacy of the flowers.

The great advantage of keeping these small things under glass is that you get them unblemished by weather, which only too often tears the petals and splashes them with mud. Besides, one often gets delightful surprises. I got one. In the autumn I had been dividing some of the 6-in. high iris *pumila*, and put some spare rhizomes into flat pans for growing on my shelf. Mysterious seedlings appeared, obviously not a weed; I left them and they developed into sturdy little plants of a viola which I take to be *Huntercombe purple*; the seeds must have been lying dormant in the soil. They flowered at the same time as the irises, making a pretty if unorthodox combination almost the same colour as the darker form of the iris *atropurpurea*, and making an equally good foil to the pale blue of iris *coerulea*. Such simple happenings give extravagant pleasure. I have a disquieting suspicion that deliberate attempts might not prove nearly so satisfactory. Nature sometimes has ideas of her own which are better than ours.

April 28, 1957

I wonder how many people visited the Alpine Garden Society's show in the R.H.S. Old Hall at the beginning of this month? Admittedly, many of the exquisite exhibits in this specialized branch of gardening are too rare and difficult for the average grower, but nearly every amateur has some kind of rock-garden, be it only a stone trough, as a sanctuary for small treasures, and a dozen suggestions may be picked up and profitably pursued. The advantage of rock-gardening is that it may be on any scale, from a disused quarry to a few stones put together in such a way as to supply pockets for the appropriate soil; segregation of colonies where the little plants may display their individuality without the rivalry of a coarser neighbour; and what gardeners call a cool root-run for certain Alpines which enjoy burrowing under boulders in as near an approximation as possible to conditions in their native hills.

It is a hobby for the rich man and the poor man alike.

It is, however, not always easy to decide what to grow, especially in a limited space, and not always easy to discover where to obtain the rarity one covets. For this reason, and considering the very wide appeal that rock-gardening makes, the enthusiast would be well advised not only to visit these shows (which are held also at places other than London) but also to join the Society outright. The annual subscription of £1 entitles the member to the admirable *Quarterly Bulletin*, illustrated, a small volume in itself, of about 100 pages, which to non-members costs 5s. a copy or £1 a year, and which contains articles written for both the expert and the beginner. I pick, haphazard, a few titles from recent issues: 'Alpines worth growing'; 'Let's make a rock-garden'; 'Some bulbous plants for the rock-garden'; 'Visits to the Upper Engadine'; 'August in the rock-garden,' and so on, perhaps enough to suggest that there is something for all tastes.

Furthermore, the member may borrow books from the Society's library, free of charge and paying only the postage. Finally, he will find pages of Alpine nurserymen's adver-

tisements with addresses, a most useful guide for the perplexed. There is also a seed-distribution scheme for the
benefit of members.

The address of the Society's Secretary is C. B. Saunders,
Esq., Husseys, Green Street Green, Farnborough, Kent.

April 29, 1956

I have sometimes amused myself by making miniature
gardens. The ones I made were usually meant to be given
to an invalid for a few weeks of entertainment in an
imprisoned life. Serious gardeners will certainly condemn
them as a frivolous form of gardening. I agree. You can't
take them seriously, but you can have a lot of minor fun
and pleasure so long as it lasts. I suggest also that it is quite
a good way to start an interest in very young people; the
ten-year-old, naturally impatient, can get an instant effect
without digging up his plants to see how they are growing.

The container will be the first consideration. A wooden
box, an old saucepan, or an outsize Alpine pan, will all do,
remembering that a hole or holes for drainage are essential,
with a layer of crocks all over the bottom to prevent the
soil from making its escape. The soil itself should be what
gardeners call 'open,' that is, loose and porous enough not
to cake, but also rich enough to provide sustenance in com-
pensation for its shallowness. Some handfuls of bone-meal
will prove as safe a food as anything, mixed in with fibrous
loam, some well-rotted leaf-mould or horticultural peat,
some grit or sharp sand to help the 'open-ness,' and perhaps
some bits of charcoal to keep it sweet. Fibrous loam can be
obtained from the top spit of a meadow, or from a heap of
rotted turves; I won't suggest going to the elaborate length
of sterilizing it, but do at least rub it through a wire sieve
to eliminate the risk of any perennial weeds.

What you will plant must depend upon the size at your
disposal and upon your own ideas and desires. Obviously

the things must all be tiny or they will look out of proportion. Here are a few suggestions. Small-flowered saxifrages
such as *S. irvingii*; *Arenaria balearica*; *mentha requieni*;
the Alpine poppy, *Papaver alpinum*; *narcissus nanus*; the
pink daisy *Bellis Dresden China*; the little thrift *Armeria
corsica*; and, for an annual which renews itself self-sown,
the pigmy violet Cress burdened with the appallingly
heavy name of *Ionopsidium acaule*. Some of the sedums
and sempervivums are practically foolproof if you will forgive me the word: I was thinking of very young and
interfering fingers.

I could go on for pages. I have, for instance, said nothing
about the layout of the miniature garden; pools and rivers
made of looking-glass; lawns made of moss; paved paths;
and bits of stone to represent rocks. There are so many
possibilities. I might return to the subject if it finds favour
with readers of *The Observer* and if they will promise not
to put gnomes, elves, or toadstools into their miniature
gardens, but to make them as natural as possible, like the
reflection of a full-sized garden seen through the wrong end
of a telescope.

May

May 5, 1957

I think I shall soon have to stop writing these articles, because I see that they are becoming like a parody of my own style. *Punch* takes them off, which is a compliment in its way. What really worries me is that I can't write otherwise. I do not, for instance, know how to describe the dwarf April-flowering irises except in my own terms, and that will sound very much like a take-off, and will give perhaps an exaggerated picture of the little irises I mean.

Iris pumila and *chamœiris* are well known: we have all grown them for years, and if we haven't we should. I shall not bother you with the botanical differences between the two. For the average gardener they can safely go under the same name. And how pretty and easy they are: stumpy little irises coming up amongst stumpy leaves. They flower so generously, and lend themselves so readily to division and increase of their rhizomes. If you have one, you can make two; and if you have a dozen, you can make two dozen, splitting them up and replanting directly after they have flowered.

What people perhaps don't realize is that there is now available a whole lot of named varieties of these small irises. They go under fancy names: Mist o' pink, The Bride, Amber Queen, Orange Queen, Blue Lagoon, Burgundy, Mauve Mist, and many others, all desirable. They vary in height from 6 to 8 in., and in price from 1s. 6d. to 15s., the average price being about 2s. *Mist o' Pink* seems expensive at 5s., but is one of the loveliest; *Cyanea*, blue, is cheap at 1s. 6d., and scented into the bargain. I am attracted by the name *The Great Smokies*, described as a smoky red-purple 8 in., 2s. 6d., but I have never seen it in flower, Sentimentalists may be attracted by *Tiny Treasure*, yellow, 6 in., 5s.

There are many places where all these tinies may be grown. On the top of a dry-wall; in the rock-garden; flourishing in troughs or in a flagged path where they seem particularly happy, getting their roots under the cool cover of the stone, or grown on a raised bed where they get the drainage they like. All they ask is a sunny open place and good drainage. Some people like to grow them in a wide band along the front of a border, as an edging, much as you might use pinks or thrift. This arrangement never appeals to me, personally, because I think their small delicacy is lost in conjunction with the stronger oncoming growth of herbaceous plants; to show up to their best, they need an otherwise bare place to themselves. I fancy, however, that they would associate very prettily with some of the miniature or fairy roses; their scale would be in accordance.

This is the time to order and obtain the little irises. The Orpington Nurseries, Crofton Lane, Orpington, Kent, have a long list.

May 7, 1956

The lovely race of the wind-flowers, or anemones, began with the florist's tight bunches of *St. Brigid* and *de Caen* from Cornwall and the Scillies in January, succeeded towards the end of March by the starry blue Greek, *blanda*, and the blue Italian, *apennina*, succeeded by our own white *nemerosa* in the woods. I know that I have several times written about the wind-flowers in this column, but cannot help returning to so delectable a subject.

In the seventeenth century they were called by the charming name of Parsley Roses, because of their fringed and curly leaves.

Many people complain that they cannot get anemones to do well. I think this may be due to two or three causes. Planting the corms too deep is a very common reason for failure. One and a half to two inches is quite deep enough. Another mistake frequently made is to buy the large-size corms in preference to the smaller, in the very natural belief that top-sizes, known as Jumbos in the trade, will give finer flowers. The reverse is true. Avoid Jumbo.

It should also be remembered that most anemones like an alkaline soil, which should be good news for the lime dwellers. An exception, of course, is the woodland *nemerosa* and its varieties *robinsoniana* and *alleni*; but you have only to think of our other native, *Anemone pulsatilla*, to realize that it occurs in its natural state on the chalky Downs. I am not saying that anemones will thrive only in soil where lime is present; in my own garden, for instance, where the soil, thank God, is neutral, many of them sow themselves all over the place, even in the grass of an orchard; but I do suggest that if your anemones disappoint you might well consider giving them a top dressing of lime.

Another thing that amateur growers do not always realize is that anemones of the *St. Brigid* and *de Caen* strain will not persist for ever. One has to renew after two or three years, but as non-Jumbo corms cost only 12s. to 13s. a thousand they should be well within the purse of anybody who would like to share the thousand out among friends.

Anemone fulgens, on the other hand, the brilliant red wind-flower of Mediterranean coasts, may be left for years in the same place and indeed dislikes being dug up. I think the same would apply to its descendant, the *St. Bavo* anemone, which sows itself in cracks of pavement and comes up year after year in ever more varying colours.

I often wonder why people don't grow the *St. Bavo*. They don't seem to know about it, and are surprised when they see it, with its subtle colour of petals with an electric-blue blotch at the base.

There is so much more I could say about anemones, so much much more, but if you want to learn more I must refer you to a new book called *Anemones*, by Roy Genders, published by Faber and Faber, 12s. 6d.

May 8, 1955

Interest is being increasingly taken in vermiculite, so although I do not know very much about it I think I should at least be fulfilling a duty in mentioning it. Such a nice clean thing to handle, beige in colour, like the finest possible oatmeal, with little shiny bits of mica to brighten it up.

This up-to-date aid to horticulture is made of mica, an ore which is mined in the United States, in South Africa, in Uruguay and Uganda.

Terrible things are done to it before it comes into our hands: it gets heated up to 2,000 degrees Fahrenheit to make it expand, I hope not so painful a process as it sounds. Thus expanded or exfoliated, it becomes featherweight and incredibly absorbent of moisture; in fact, from the driest oatmeal it will take on all the characteristics of a sponge that does not dry out.

Its primary use at present for the majority of amateurs is for propagation by means of cuttings, which are said to root in it more easily than in other forms of compost. It should first be thoroughly soaked in water, and then squeezed out as far as possible, when it is unlikely that you will have to moisten it again before the cuttings have taken root. Do not leave them in the vermiculite longer than necessary, since it provides no nourishment for the new little plants, but set them out to grow on in the soil or compost you would normally use. They may suffer a slight check after this transplanting, but that is nothing to worry about.

It can be used to fill seed-boxes or pots, or to make up a bed in a frame, according to the quantity you are prepared to buy and the quantity of cuttings you wish to strike.

You should be careful to get a brand where the pH value is stated, as obviously too alkaline or too acid a content would disagree with some cuttings. The neutral pH 7 is best, and the kind called Ex-flor is recommended.

Vermiculite may be used many times over, thus making it more economical than might appear at first sight.

It must be understood that vermiculite is still at an experimental stage, though it has been known to advanced horticulturists for about ten years. Too expensive at present for amateur use except on a modest scale, considerable possibilities are claimed for it in the improvement and aeration of soils, especially lawns; in the cultivation of tomatoes and mushrooms; in the raising of lilies from seed and scales; and for use in tubs and window-boxes, owing to the extreme lightness compared with a filling of ordinary soil. Only, if you decide to try it for this purpose, you must supply nourishment in the form of liquid manure, remembering that vermiculite is merely a rooting medium and contains nothing of food value.

It is certainly worth a trial when the time for taking cuttings comes round. It would be interesting to set one batch in the sandy misture you habitually use, and a similar batch in vermiculite, and watch the results.

May 12, 1957

It was borne in on me, not for the first time, how the weeds of one country are the flowers of another. Recently, in the tropics, I had been shocked on seeing my host and hostess as they wandered round their garden tearing up

green oddments as we should tear up groundsel, saying,
'That wretched thing! All over the place as usual!' This was
Gloriosa superba, which we have to grow carefully in heat
if we want it at all.

I do not want to grow *Gloriosa superba*, but I must admit
to having been rather pleased with a combination on my
house-wall of *Ceanothus dentatus* and *Solanum crispum*.
They both come out at the same time, and I thought the
mauve flowers of the climbing potato-vine mixed very
agreeably with the powder-blue of the ceanothus. I have
always lived in terror lest some dreadful winter should
murder the lot, but although the ceanothus took a nasty
knock in February 1956, they have all so far survived, and
I would recommend anyone desirous of covering his house-
wall in a smoke of blue and mauve in April and May to
reproduce this idea I so proudly had.

Why proudly? One should never be too proud. One
gets taken down. A most gentle and charming lady from
California came into my garden and looked at the ceanothus.* 'Now isn't that pretty?' she said, 'and to think
those things grow all over our woods and we never think
of using them like that. Just weeds they are, with us.
Now look at your hyacinths, all along your banks and in
your woods, we couldn't ever grow them by the acre like
that.'

I realized that by hyacinths she meant what we in England commonly though incorrectly call bluebells, and did
indeed agree that no one could plant a bluebell wood deliberately, not even if he were a millionaire and could employ
a thousand gardeners. Even so, it would not look the same
as our natural woods are looking just now:

> A juicy and a jostling shock
> Of bluebells sheaved in May.

* *Solanum crispum* is a native of Chile, not of California.

The weeds of one country are indeed the flowers of another. How kindly we should smile if we saw a bed carefully planted with bluebells somewhere in Illinois or Missouri. I hope only that our smiles would be as tolerant as those of my visitor from California, looking at the ceanothus which to her was a weed.

May 13, 1956

Everybody is still busy assessing the damage caused by February's atrocious jokes. I am sure it is wise not to despair of any plant until one is quite quite certain that it is quite quite dead. Already, even before one sees little green proofs of life reviving, a sliver taken off by a penknife reveals soft green under the brown bark. One gets surprises, some unpleasant but some pleasant. The pleasant are usually connected with the reputed hardiness or non-hardiness of the plant concerned.

Our ideas on this subject have to be constantly revised. In an old nursery catalogue of nearly a hundred years ago I find *Alstroemeria ligtu* advertised as suitable for the hothouse, and the hardy little *cyclamen repandum* for the greenhouse. *Alstroemeria aurantiaca*, the common yellow Peruvian lily, long since discarded as too invasive a weed and seldom seen now except in a wild corner or in cottage gardens, is also recommended for the greenhouse. Such misapprehensions make us smile, but I fancy we should not be too superior and should humbly remember that we still have much to learn. I learnt a lot from February 1956, and from previous experiences. I am now convinced that it is as important to wrap the ankles, legs, and thighs of woody growth as to protect the shoulders and head with hessian or other covering. Warm gaiters of sacking, bound round with string, may prevent the bark from being torn asunder by frost or the trunk itself from splitting, a fatal injury never to be survived. I would instance an old lemon verbena

growing in my garden for many years. This year, for the
first time, we covered it entirely; and can I find any sign
of life in it? I cannot. It did much better with a heap of
ashes over its feet, a gaiter of straw-stuffed sacking up its
shins and its top left to take all risks for itself.

On the whole, I think this past winter has been less
destructive than the winter of 1946–47. That was the
winter when we got the ice-rain, and all our shrubs became
coated with ice and turned into frozen beards against the
house-wall, or tinkled like glass chandeliers in the open,
stirred by the breeze, and the boughs of the trees themselves became iridescent as the low rays of the sun struck
them; and the puzzled birds, trying to perch, skidded up
and down, finding no claw-hold.

We were spared this, in 1956, and I still feel optimistic,
even about *Caryopteris clandonensis*, which threatened to
desert me for ever, and a ceanothus which would have been
a serious loss.

May 15, 1955

The more I prowl round my garden at this time of year,
especially during that stolen hour of half-dusk between tea
and supper, the more do I become convinced that a great
secret of good gardening lies in covering every patch of the
ground with some suitable carpeter. Much as I love the
chocolate look of the earth in winter, when spring comes
back I always feel that I have not done enough, not nearly
enough, to plant up the odd corners with little low things
that will crawl about, keeping weeds away, and tuck
themselves into chinks that would otherwise be devoid of
interest or prettiness.

The violets, for instance—I would not despise even our
native *Viola odorata* of the banks and hedgerows, either
in its blue or its white form, so well deserving the adjective
odorata. And how it spreads, wherever it is happy, so why

not let it roam and range as it listeths? (I defy a
to pronounce that word.) There are other v
choice than our wildling; the little pink *Coe*
or *Viola labradorica*, for instance, which from
roots planted last year is now making huge clumps and
bumps of purplish leaf and wine-coloured flower, and is
sowing itself all over the place wherever it is wanted or
not wanted. It is never not wanted, for it can be lifted and
removed to another place, where it will spread at its good
will.

There are many other carpeters beside the violets, some
for sunny places and some for shade. For sunny places the
thymes are perhaps unequalled, but the sunny places are
never difficult to fill. Shady corners are more likely to worry
the gardener trying to follow my advice of cram, cram,
cram every chink and cranny. *Arenaria balearica* loves a
dark, damp home, especially if it can be allowed to crawl
adhesively over mossy stones. On a dark green mat it
produces masses of what must be one of the tinest flowers,
pure white, starry; an easy-going jewel for the right
situation. *Cotula squalida* is much nicer than its name: it
is like a miniature fern, and it will spread widely and will
help to keep the weeds away.

The *Acaenas* will likewise spread widely, and should do
well in shade; they have bronzy-coloured leaves and crawl
neatly over their territory. The list of carpeters is endless,
and I wish I had enough space to amplify these few
suggestions. The one thing I feel sure of is that every odd
corner should be packed with something permanent,
something of interest and beauty, something tucking itself
into something else in the natural way of plants when they
sow themselves and combine as we never could combine
them with all our skill and knowledge.

May 19, 1957

There is a family of plants so easy to grow, so diverse in their character and their interest, that I wonder they are not more freely used in our gardens. I mean the great family of the euphorbias, said to contain over one thousand members. The grandest of them is *Euphorbia pulcherrima*, which we know better under the familiar name of poinsettia, but that is not a plant for anybody without a hot greenhouse.

Other euphorbias are for anybody with an ordinary garden. Would it sound less alarming if I called them by their English name, spurge? There are about a dozen native to this island, from the common wood spurge, which is well worth growing in a rough place as a ground cover under trees if you do not fear it as an invader, to the queerly handsome caper spurge, upright as a little column. Factually an annual, it seeds itself so generously and has a habit of placing itself just where it knows it will look best, as though it were possessed of some natural architectural sense, that you need never bother about sowing it afresh.

I am very fond of *Euphorbia marginata*, unfortunately an annual, and unfortunately attractive to sparrows. They peck. I persist, however, for the sake of the green-and-silver effect of the striped leaves and the white bracts. If the caper spurge has an architectural quality, *Euphorbia marginata* has an heraldic quality: it might be dressed in a tabard. It is a native of the southern states of North America, where it is known as Snow-on-the-mountain.

I am very fond also of *Euphorbia pilosa*. This is a perennial, and grows in a neat little rounded clump of greenish-gold, about a foot high. It is at its best in spring, but very tidy all the year round. I had it once in association with the greenish viola *Irish Molly*, and a very happy association it was. Molly died on me, but the spurge heartlessly shows every sign of increasing in vigour.

The most exciting spurge I have got is called *Eu,*
griffithii. It was collected in Tibet, and was given an
of Merit a couple of years ago. It has the strangest
bination of colouring: brown, orange and green, givi.
general impression of rusty red, not unlike *Euphorbia*
sikkimensis. Please, try this if you don't already know it.
You can get it from Miss Davenport-Jones, Washfield
Nurseries, Hawkhurst, Kent. One root of it will rush all
over the place within twelve months, so the 3s. 6d. you
might have to expend on one root will pay 100 per cent
dividend. I am not good at sums, but I do know that
Euphorbia griffithii increases almost at compound interest.

Then there is *Euphorbia wulfenii*. I have never grown
this, and I don't like to recommend plants without personal
experience of them, but I realize that *E. wulfenii* is a
serious lapse on my part. It must be one of the most recommendable of the spurges.

The Stocklands Estate Nursery, Bewdley, Worcestershire,
has an imposing list.

NOTE: I must add a word of warning. Two correspondents have reminded me that some people are allergic to the white juice exuded by
euphorbias and one of them has mentioned even, quoting from an
old book, that 'African and American savages tip their arrows with
the deadly poison.' I hope that this alarming statement will not put
anybody off. The obvious moral is never to cut or break the stem, and
to handle the plant with gloves if you anticipate the slightest risk. A
similar white juice exuded by the stalk of fig-leaves is said to be a cure
for warts, dabbed on, a drop to a wart, so doubtless some corrosive
acid is present in both cases.

May 20, 1956

Owners of the four big volumes of the Royal Horticultural Society's encyclopædic *Dictionary of Gardening* will
want to add the supplementary volume which appeared last
week under the editorship of Mr. Patrick Synge with the
assistance of Mr. Lanning Roper and many experts. It costs
42s. and is published by the Clarendon Press, Oxford.

£1 17s. 6d. carriage paid to Fellows and Associates of the R.H.S.

The supplement contains many articles on subjects largely ignored in the four previous volumes, and in this respect may be regarded as bringing the great Dictionary more up to date. Thus there are sections devoted to long lists of the most desirable and reliable varieties of fruit, vegetables, flowers, etc., reading more like a nurseryman's catalogue, or, to put it differently, taking a less highbrow attitude. This was a good idea. After all, we don't all aspire to grow *Ornithocephalus tonduzii* or *Phyllocladus rhomboidalis*, but some of us do like to be told about potatoes and runner beans, and some of us like to be told about the latest types of Floribunda rose. Incidentally, I must register a not-small grievance against this momentous publication. It takes insufficient notice of the shrubby 'old' roses, recently revived into favour and rescued from many a Victorian garden, the rose of Provins, the Gallicas, the Damasks, the centifolias. They get a mention, but I think they should have been granted an entry all to themselves. Owners of the Dictionary, aware of this deficiency, had better secure without delay a copy of *The Old Shrub Roses*, by Graham Thomas, the most authoritative and comprehensive book so far written on the subject. (Phoenix House, 32s. 6d.)

The articles about disease and pest control, compost heaps, fertilizers, and what plants want from the soil, will all be full of interest to the scientifically minded gardener. There is something for everybody in this supplement, amateurs or experts. It shows what a lot there is to be learnt about the huge subject of gardening, and shows that the more one learns the more there is to learn. It leaves me feeling like a five-year-old beginning to put letters of the alphabet together, the cat-on-the-mat, the dog-and-the-rat, with no conception of the vast landscape opening out beyond.

Vast landscapes of possibilities in our gardens, even on

a small scale. This is always an exciting idea. One must go ahead with experiments, and not stand still. One must always try out new things, such as *Venidio-arctotis*, now blazing orange stars in my garden.

May 22, 1955

I was amused to read a paragraph two or three weeks ago from the Washington Correspondent of *The Observer* about the Multiflora rose which is now being planted so extensively in the United States along the sides of main roads and also on the strip between dual highways. It was described in that paragraph as a safety net, being resilient enough to arrest even a ton-and-a-half lorry bumping into it at speed. You can bounce back and come to a standstill with no damage to yourself or your vehicle beyond a few scratches on the paint.

I had heard of this peculiar buffer some time ago, but I did not make an *In Your Garden* article about it because I knew it was not procurable in this country, and nothing is more annoying than being given a tempting description of a plant one cannot obtain. As, however, it has now been publicly mentioned, and in my own *Observer* to boot, I thought I might now allow myself to expand on this most interesting subject. Besides, it will be procurable in this country before long, in the form of seedlings which are already coming up like mustard and cress in a rosarian's nursery. I had the good fortune to be sent some seeds by a generous American friend, and passed some of them on to Miss Hilda Murrell, of the Portland Nurseries, Shrewsbury, who tells me that she has obtained 100 per cent germination.

It does sound the most extraordinarily boastful sort of rose hedge. It can be had in a thornless or a thorny form. The thorny form sounds terrifying, as described in the American leaflet: 'Horse-high; Bull-strong; Goat-tight;

thick and cruel enough to keep out any form of marauding live-stock,' and in addition to all this it grows six to eight feet high, smothered in small white flowers, sometimes a very pale pink. The State of Missouri has planted 3,000 miles of this rose along its roads during the last five years. We do not plant on this scale in this small island. I wish we did. Our main roads might then take on a new character, not tar-macadam bleak, but bordered by rose-hedges combining beauty with utility.

The Americans claim also that the multiflora rose requires no maintenance, pruning, training, or support; is long-lived; resistant to wind; rapid of growth, four to five feet in a season; and makes an excellent cover for wild life. I must say that the photographs in the leaflet are startlingly impressive.

May 26, 1957

The reproach sometimes reaches me of writing only for owners of very spacious, ancient, romantic gardens, with century-old hedges of yew and holly, fountains spouting into marble basins, flanked by tritons, mermaids and sportive dolphins, lawns of turf as pure as a putting-green, Cedars of Lebanon mirrored in pools of translucent water inhabited by ancestral carp with golden rings in their noses.

I do, in fact, try to bear every type of garden in mind, and to think especially of the owners of a brand-new garden who don't know what to do with it so let me recommend two books: *Your New Garden*, by A. G. L. Hellyer, 18s. (Collingridge), and *The New Small Garden*, by Lady Allen of Hurtwood and Susan Jellicoe (The Architectural Press, 15s.). Mr. Hellyer's book is the more comprehensive and practical of the two, but both are rich in ideas.

This leads me on to say that however tiny the area, something imaginative can be made out of it. Scope is not a question of acres, it is a question of taste, vision, design, colour-sense and grouping. Impossible to lay down rules since every site presents its own problem of shape, size, aspect, contour, relation to the house, locality, soil, configuration of slope or level and the owner's purse. That is why I mentioned the two books with their many photographic illustrations, rather than attempt a dogmatic dissertation on what ought or ought not to be done with a raw and presumably small garden.

Still, there are some general principles. For example, a well-placed dark little upright tree such as an Irish yew or a juniper will often give dignity by bringing the eye to a stop just where a rest is needed. Then, straight lines of paths and borders usually give a greater impression of length and distance than the weak, wavy, wobbly lines that some people consider artistic. (To deal successfully with the wavy and wobbly demands a real artist.) This, of course, does not apply to the cottage-garden, all a flurry of flowers and a paved perplexity of paths, probably the loveliest type of small garden this country has ever evolved. Above all I would suggest that if you have a lawn, you should not fuss it up with kidney-shaped beds, or, indeed, with any beds at all. We grumble at our climate, but it does give us incomparable turf, and we should leave it in a green, uninterrupted table for the repose of our eyes and souls.

May 27, 1956

Last week (see pp. 77–8) in this miserably restricted column I attempted to say something about the recently published supplementary volume to the Royal Horticultural Society's huge Dictionary of Gardening. I would have liked to add a note on the article devoted to the nomenclature or naming of plants, but I hadn't room. So I return to the subject.

This seems to be a subject calculated to arouse the silliest type of irritation in amateur gardeners. They get cross. Their crossness divides itself into two separate categories. They resent the fact that plants have Latin names, and, perhaps more understandably, that the name of a plant should so frequently be changed. The first grievance is both parochial and indefensible, postulating, as it does, that every gardener and botanist in the world must be assumed to know English. There are quite a lot of very good gardeners and botanists in Europe, Asia, Africa and South America who are as ignorant of our language as we are of theirs. Must we, then, be so insular as to reject Latin as a *lingua franca* intelligible to all? Besides, if you know a little elementary Latin, which I am sorry to say I don't, or so elementary as to be scarcely perceptible even through a magnifying-glass, you will find it a great help towards identification. I can, for instance, grasp that *aurea* means golden, and that *lutea* means a paler yellow, or that *acaulis* means short-stalked, or that *stoloniferus* means increase by runners. Any Icelandic, Nepalese, or Patagonian gardener would be as instantly and thoroughly apprised as I.

With the second grievance I can't help having a certain sympathy. I know with my rational mind that I am being unreasonably annoyed when, having mastered names such as *Tricuspidaria hookeriana*, I have to change over to *Crinodendron lanceolatum*. The R.H.S. supplement provides the explanation of these apparently freakish tactics on the part of our botanists. The aim of the Thirteenth International Horticultural Congress, 1952, was to 'promote uniformity, accuracy and fixity in the use of names and to debar or discourage procedures leading to confusion and error.' An effort was then made to restore the correct scientific name, and that correct name must be 'the earliest available name which is in accordance with the system of classification and the international rules of nomenclature accepted at the time,' or, in other words, 'the earliest legitimate name.' This, of course, is putting the matter far too simply for so complicated a subject, and many modifications have still to be introduced. I must refer anyone interested to the somewhat formidable article on pages 271 to 278 of the R.H.S. supplement.

No doubt everything will be adjusted in time, and our descendants will no longer have any cause for indignation.

May 29, 1955

This is to recommend a shrub startling to the eye in spring, for it then presents the richest reddest coloration of autumn. People blink in unbelief when they first espy the dark green bush tipped with scarlet. They mistake the poinsettia-red tips for an inflorescence, but on going closer discover that they are in fact the young shoots of leaves, fiery, pointed, glossy, and looking as though they had some artificial lighting behind them.

This is *Pieris forrestii*, named after George Forrest, who first found it growing wild in the Yunnan province of China.

Of all the *piereses*, Forrest's is the most magnificent. *Pieris japonica* is good enough, but Forrest's far excels it. He must have been surprised when he came across it blazing on the slopes of its native mountains. The nib of Farrer's pen would have struck such sparks as to kindle his whole page into a bonfire. Unfortunately Forrest lacked the descriptive powers of Reginald Farrer, and is content to remark merely that it is 'a most excellent shrub,' finer than any of its class he has seen.

It was first shown at Chelsea in 1924, so is a fairly recent acquisition for our gardens.

I have expatiated on the beauty of the young shoots, which indeed is the glory of this plant, but the flowers also have their charm. They come in hanging clusters of creamy little bells, at the same time as the young shoots, so that the whole plant in April or May gives an effect of dark green, bright red, and pale tassels.

It has its drawbacks—what plant hasn't? Belonging as it does to the botanical family of the ericaceae, it is a lime-hater. You can grow it safely in any soil where rhododendrons, azaleas, or kalmias flourish, or you can make up a peaty bed for it with lots of leaf-mould, but it will have nothing to say to an alkaline or chalky soil. Another of its dislikes is cold winds and who shall blame it? Finally, it dislikes late spring frosts, but again who shall blame it? We can, however, arrange to protect our plants better than we can arrange to protect ourselves: we have to move about, whatever the weather, whereas our plants are static and it is up to us, their masters, to place them in the position that suits them best. A hurdle stuffed with straw or bracken will do much to defend them against the prevailing wind. Many of us would have been glad to cower, during the early weeks of May this year, behind so kind and cosy a stockade.

June

June 2, 1957

A NY well-trained journalist would pick out the high-lights of the Chelsea Show. I cannot be a well-trained journalist since I always miss the things everybody else has noticed and notice the things nobody else takes any interest in. There were, however, three or four oddments which caught my eye amongst the mass of shrubs, annuals, rock plants, overgrown begonias and cauliflowers.

There was a new poppy from Nepal, of a colour comparable only to the breast of a chaffinch. Moreover the unopened buds were covered in tiny golden hairs, which at first sight I mistook for pollen, imagining that it should not be grown in the open lest the rain should smear the gilded dust in the same way as it smears the farina on some auriculas. This poppy should be acquired by all gardeners who can succeed with the lovely family of meconopsis. I was told that seed would be available next year.* It should be an exciting plant to grow from seed, judging by the pale pink seedling shown on the same stall. One would never know what one was going to get.

Then, I was delighted to see the old double petunia revived. Messrs. Sutton showed it. Curly as parsley, it took me right back to my childhood. Perhaps it was sentimental of me to have been so moved at the sight of this forgotten

---

* Mr. H. G. Lyall, who showed these poppies, tells me that he now (1958) has a limited number of seedlings available. His address will be found on page 196 of this book.

object, but why should one not allow oneself the luxury of being sentimental sometimes?

A much queerer object struck me in Messrs. Rochfort's collection of house-plants. This was *Vriesia splendens*. It looked as though some medieval clerk had dipped the feathered end of his quill-pen into blood and then stuck it upright into the heart of green-and-silver leaves, as into an ink-horn.

If you think of getting a *Vriesia*, don't let it come under a hot sun. It burns.

June 3, 1956

Three short disparate paragraphs this week, instead of a consecutive article.

The first paragraph concerns the lifting of bulbs, such as tulips, and heeling them in until the time comes for replanting them next autumn. I think myself that their journey is unnecessary. I have had tulips growing in the same place without disturbance for at least ten years, and they show little sign of deterioration. Perhaps the flower is not as large as it once was, but who wants exhibition tulips except on the show-bench? I leave my tulips in, and let them take their chance, and they reward me by taking it. I do, however, realize that in a small garden they may have to be cleared out to make room for other things; and since this is the time to lift them I thought I would pass on an ingenious hint given to me by an inventive old countryman. 'You heel them in in their trench,' he said, 'and then later on they die down and it's difficult to find them and anyhow you've forgotten which sort was which. But if you put a length of mesh-wire along the bottom of the trench, with a label tied on to it saying what sorts they are, all you have to do is to pull up the wire and the bulbs come up with it, and then you know what you've got.' This seems a most practical and commendable suggestion, but it would have to be the kind of label that doesn't rot. Not a paper label.

The second paragraph concerns a book. It is a book written by a woman who, with her husband, created out of nothing the sort of garden we should all like to have, a cottage garden on a slightly larger scale than the average cottage garden. This one in Somerset is just under an acre in extent. The book is crammed with good advice, even as the author's garden is obviously crammed with good plants —ordinary plants, interesting plants, and plants grown just for their suitability irrespective of whether they are rare or common, so long as they look right where they are and fulfil their function in the garden-picture. Failures and successes are recorded with equal honesty. I defy any amateur gardener not to find pleasure, encouragement and profit from *We Made a Garden*, by Margery Fish (Collingridge, 18s.), generously illustrated by photographs.

In my third paragraph I must allow myself a purple patch. It isn't purple at all: it is blue. Blue as the Mediterranean on a calm day; blue as the smoke rising in autumn bonfires from our autumnal woods; blue seen through the young green of chestnut or beech; blue as the star-cabochon sapphire given to a bride on her wedding-day; hyacinth-scented beyond all these, just a bluebell wood, an ordinary thing, a thing we take for granted.

June 5, 1955

Many people hesitate to plant that most noble of flowering trees, the magnolia, under the impression that they will never live long enough or remain for long enough in the same place to see it flower. It is true that some kinds of magnolia are not suitable for a short-term tenancy. *Magnolia campbelli*, for instance, may demand twenty-five years before it pays any dividend on its original cost. But this is not true of some other kinds.

The Yulan tree, once known as *M. conspicua* but now called *M. denudata*, produces a few of its creamy chalices within a year or two of planting, and increases in size and fertility until it is one hundred years old or more. I planted one twenty years ago, and it has long since achieved a height of 20 ft. and a spread of 15 ft. So you see. Its only serious enemy, very serious indeed, is a March frost which may turn its candid purity to a leathery khaki brown. Sometimes it escapes; one must take the risk; it is worth taking.

M. stellata, which also flowers in extreme youth, is perhaps the most familiar of all the magnolias to be seen in the amateur gardener's garden. To my way of thinking, it is by no means one of the most beautiful, being ragged and tattered-looking, but a well-grown bush is certainly effective, seen at a distance.

M. salicifolia is one of the easiest and hardiest, and its flowers are less susceptible to frost than either the Yulan or *M. stellata*, but if you want to get away from the white varieties you can have the hybrid *M. lennei*, huge rosy flowers in late April and May, or its relation, *M. rustica-rubra*, slightly deeper in colour and stouter in shape. Or, if you want something really sumptuous, there is the claret-coloured *M. liliflora nigra*, which in my experience flowers continuously for nearly two months, May and June; it is a good plant for small gardens, as it grows neither too high nor too wide, and I have never known it fail to flower copiously every year.

This is a shockingly short article to devote to so magnificent and important a genus; I have not even mentioned that the magnolia is easygoing as to soil; likes some peat or leaf-mould but does not exact it; appreciates a rich mulch from time to time; is rather brittle and thus prefers a sheltered to a windy position; and should be transplanted in spring (March) rather than in autumn. It so happens, however, that a great book on the Asiatic magnolias has

just been published, representing notes taken over thirty
years by one of our finest gardeners, Mr. G. H. Johnstone,
a holder of the coveted V.M.H., the highest award that the
Royal Horticultural Society can offer. From this book you
can learn more about magnolias than anyone else is likely
to tell you.

Asiatic Magnolias in Cultivation. By G. H. Johnstone,
R.H.S., Vincent Square, S.W.1, £3 3s.

June 9, 1957

The tulips at Chelsea were magnificent and motley as
usual, and in anticipation of the autumn bulb catalogues
I made a few notes of some that especially pleased me. They
may not all be to everybody's taste, but one must have the
courage of one's own convictions.

Among the self-coloured, I thought *Palestrina* and
Prunus and *General de la Rey* would collaborate in a lovely
salmon-pink group, not sweetly pink like old *Clara Butt*,
but with just that dash of the stronger redeeming orange.
It is always difficult to describe colours, especially as the
texture of petals is a thing all on its own; you may compare
it to silks and velvets, but the luminosity is lacking in any
textile. Let us say that *Palestrina, Prunus,* and *General de
la Rey* resemble smoked salmon, if you can imagine
smoked salmon sliced into wafers so thin that you could see
the light through them. Among the dark reds, *Indian Chief*
and *Bandoeng* are both very sombre and fine.

I love very much the broken tulips also, and don't at all
resent the idea that their feathery variation should be
caused by a virus. *Black Boy* took my fancy, but then I have
a weakness for all the Rembrandts and Bizarres and By-
bloemen which come straight out of a Dutch flower picture,
as also for the great Parrots, more numerous every year,
wilder and wilder in their tatterdemalion rags. I suppose
every tulip lover has grown *Fantasy* for years, apple-green

and pink, and probably has gone on to growing the black, the blue, the orange, the red and even the Dragon mixture. Let me add *Discovery*, old-rose and green, and *Faraday*, a white sport of Fantasy.

The Parrots are all well known, rather too large and floppy for a small garden perhaps, so I turn to a smaller and more manageable party, all neatly pretending to be made of china. Have you grown *Artist*? If not, order a few, expensive at 13s. a dozen, but still more or less of a novelty. Terra-cotta and green when it first opens, it ends its days pink, green and white. It looks strangely artificial for a Cottage tulip. *Artist* is subtle in its colouring; *Fireflame* lives up to its name. A sport of that fine old *Inglescombe Yellow*, it has added some flares of orange and red to the solid gold of its parent.

Perhaps the most sophisticated looking of these striped Cottage tulips is *viridiflora praecox*, also the most expensive, in fact horribly expensive, at 4s. 6d. each or 48s. a dozen. Let us hope that it will come down, for it is really a treasure for the connoisseur. There is a cheaper *viridiflora*, called *Greenland*, at 1s. 6d. each or 16s. 6d. a dozen; this I have not seen.* I have a feeling that the pure green-and-white of *viridiflora praecox* would be preferable. It does sometimes happen, unfortunately, that the most expensive is the best.

June 10, 1956

A friend asks me to write something about growing climbing plants up into trees. I have some recollection of having written about it before, but as it is a form of gardening particularly dear to me I welcome the suggestion and hope that nobody will mind my returning to it.

So often there is a valueless old tree in a garden, it might be an apple or one of those old pears whose fruits never get

* I have now. It is horrible.

any softer than pebbles, or even a dead tree fit only for the
woodman's axe.

> Woodman, spare that tree!
> Touch not a single bough,

as George Pope Morris appealingly wrote some time in the
last century, going on to say that in youth it had sheltered
him and therefore deserved his protection. Today, following the example of William Robinson in his once famous
garden at Gravetye, he would doubtless have used it as a
prop for some wreathing, writhing climber, as Mr. Robinson
tossed roses, honeysuckles, clematis and vines in profusion
and let them find their way upwards towards the light.
Swarthy sombre trees, say a Lawson's cypress or a thuya,
are especially suitable for such treatment, since the dark
background enhances the beauty of the climber's flower
and also gives thick and twiggy support. The familiar
macrocarpa of hedges will grow to a tree of pyramidal
shape and considerable height and, with its lower branches
trimmed away, exposing the trunk, is perhaps the best
substitute at our command for the Italian cypress. A
vigorous climber, such as *Clematis montana*, should soon
clothe it to the top; this small-flowered clematis can be had
in its white form, or in the pink variety, *rubra*. The so-
called Russian vine, *Polygonum baldschuanicum*, most rapid
of climbers, will go to a height of 20 ft. or more, and is
attractive with its feathery plumes of a creamy white. It
should scarcely be necessary to emphasize the value of the
wistarias for similar purpose.

One advantage of this use of climbers for a small garden
is the saving of ground space. The soil, however, should
be richly made up in the first instance, as the tree-roots
will rob it grossly, and will also absorb most of the moisture,
so see to it that a newly planted climber does not lack water
during its first season, before it has had time to become

established and is sending out its own roots far enough
or deep enough to get beyond the worst of the parched
area.

June 12, 1955

Surely I must have written before now about the
leisurely pleasure of growing species peonies from seed.
Leisurely because it takes four to five years before they
start to flower; pleasure because you never know exactly
what is going to turn up, and may get slight but interesting
variations. Some seed I took from a rather dull maroon-
coloured *P. delavayii* produced a child of lacquer-red. With
the usual perversity of plants, the parent survives and has
grown far too large for the position I gave it; a chaffinch
has nested in it, which is very charming, but I never
dreamt it would grow 8 ft. high. The child, which I felt
really proud of, succumbed without warning, probably
to the disease commonly called wilt. This disease, caused
by a fungus, is infectious and plants attacked by it should
be destroyed.

The lovely pale yellow *P. mlokosewitschi* also varies
slightly in the colour of its offspring. I got a greenish-yellow
one from the butter-yellow parent. These two happy
accidents should suffice to confirm my contention that it is
worth while growing the species from your own saved seed,
or from a packet of purchased seed. By the way, do not
confuse the species with the old herbaceous peony of borders
and cottage gardens. The species are far more subtle and
exquisite. If they have a fault, it is that their flowers are
more ephemeral. You can obviate this to a considerable
extent by setting your plants in broken shade, for a hot sun
will cook the flower quickly. Luckily, they prefer broken
shade, and this alone makes them desirable as an under-
planting for a grove of small standard trees such as the
ornamental pyrus and prunus, where the ground might

otherwise remain bare and without interest after the
blossom of the trees has gone over.

I should recommend the pale sorts rather than the
magenta colours. The pale, ghostly, papery flowers of
P. wittmaniana, whitleyi major, obovata and the white
emodi all suggest moonlight at midday. The magenta ones
are, to my thinking, too strong to mix with the wraiths.

June 16, 1957

I can't tell how you like to see tulips grown; I can tell
only how I like to see them grown myself. We must all
admire the grand displays in our public parks, especially
perhaps in the London parks crammed with a superbly
generous present of I don't know how many thousands of
bulbs from the Dutch growers a year or so ago, but that is
a thing for public parks and not for our own intimate
gardens. Taken all in all, I don't like to see tulips regi-
mented. It reminds me too much of Trooping the Colour:
one expects to see them march off in formation, wheel, and
return into smartly aligned ranks.

Nor do I much like to see tulips coming up through an
undergrowth of forget-me-not. The tulip, as I see it, is
straight and proud, hoisting its chalice high above its clean
stem. It offends me to see its gazelle-slender ankles
smothered by forget-me-not, however pretty, however
colourful, however useful, or any other fuzz.

How, then, you may ask, do I like to grow my few tulips?

The answer is that my own garden is a shockingly
unorthodox muddle. This truth was brought home to me
recently by two parties of visitors. One called it disorderly,
and the other called it casual. I saw what they both meant,
and it was the same thing. They meant that I let things
grow up haphazard and stay where they occurred, even
though I had never intended them to be there. A stray
white Darwin, solitary against an Irish yew, showed up

startlingly. Had a bulb been accidentally dropped? I shall never know. Nature sometimes betrays a divine instinct for shedding her nurslings in the right place.

My tulips are in clumps, not in straight lines. The huge yellow *Mongolia* accompanies the yellow peony *mlokose-witschi*, a deliberate piece of planting, but the Spanish yellow broom *Spartium junceum* has chosen to sow itself beside them and has been left to develop into a golden shower, disproportionate I admit, but oddly effective as they all flower at the same time. Then I planted some of the dusky red brooms, *Burkwoodii* and *Killiney Red*, quite for-getting that there was already a drift of orange-pink tulips there, and the result when they came up all amongst the brooms was surprising. The tulips glowed like a forest fire running between the dark green stems of the brooms.

I don't suggest that this untidy, disorderly, casual method would suit all gardens and all tastes, but I do suggest that it is worth consideration.

June 17, 1956

There is something in all of us which responds to some-thing we have known in our childhood. It may be a scent, or a touch, or a sight, or anything which evokes a memory. For some of us this evocation arises from the recollection of flowers we saw growing in our grandparents' gardens and now search for in vain.

Why should they have gone out of fashion, the dear old tenants of the kitchen garden border? They were not very grand, so they were usually relegated to the strip between the espalier apples and the path. They shared that strip with the old double primroses, and the Hen-and-Chicken daisy, and some Dusty Miller auriculas, all living very happily together. The plants I am thinking of now, came behind these lowly growers, into the middle-height of the border.

They all had English names by which we knew them. There was the Bleeding Heart or Lyre Flower, more familiar under that name than as *Dicentra* or *dielytra spectabilis*. One could pull each locket of the Bleeding Heart into different shapes, the most pleasing turning into a little pink-and-white ballet dancer. If you don't believe me, try it. I never say things I don't mean; or at any rate, not in this column. Then there was the Masterwort, or *Astrantia*, a greenish-white or pale pink, a reliable old plant for the border, so seldom seen now. Then there was Solomon's Seal, *Polygonatum multiflorum*; and *Smilacina racemosa*, both plants for a shady place, with grand green leaves and long strands of white moonlight flowers. The Smilacina has the advantage of a strong scent and of lasting very well in water. It deserves to be grown much more extensively.

Another old plant I like very much is *Tradescantia virginiana*, the Spiderwort named after John Tradescant, gardener to Charles I and Henrietta Maria. It is also called the Trinity Flower, owing to its three petals of a rich violet, curiously lurking amongst the grassy leaves. Perfectly hardy, it has a very long flowering season from June onwards into the autumn. It likes the sun, but will also put up with some shade. Do not confuse it with another Tradescantia, which is a trailing plant for the greenhouse, with green-and-white striped leaves.

*   *   *

I don't know how many people grow Camassia, but those who don't should. 'What is that pale blue red-hot-poker?' somebody asked me. The answer was *Camassia cusickii*, the Quamash of the North American Indians, who eat the bulbs. My reason for mentioning it here, where it may seem rather out of place amongst old herbaceous plants, is that I am advised to save the seed and sow it broadcast in rough grass, when in about four years' time I am assured that I shall get a crop as mistily blue as a sea of bluebells. It should be sown as soon as ripe; just chucked down, no need even to scratch it in. I wonder; but having been successful in a similar experiment with crocuses, I certainly intend to try.

June 19, 1955

How sumptuous are some of the modern irises! Not all flowers, in my opinion, are the better for their so-called improvement, but there can be no question about the advance of the iris at the hands of the hybridizer. It was always a flower which depended on colour and texture for its chief beauty; even the common old Germanica, so useful in sooty town gardens, relied on its imperial purple for its popularity. No adjective, however lyrical, can exaggerate the soft magnificence of the moderns, rivalled only by the texture of Genoese velvet. We have to go back to the Italian Renaissance to produce a flower as soft, as rich, as some of those velvets one used to buy for next to nothing in Venice and Rome, years ago, when one was young and scraps of velvet went cheap. Only the pansy, amongst other flowers, shares this particular quality.

Stately in their bearing, the irises look their best on either side of a flagged path. The grey of the flat stone sets off both their colour and their contrasting height. I have never made up my mind whether the paths should be straight or curved. A straight path gives an effect of regimental parade, which suits the irises, whose leaves suggest uplifted swords. On the other hand, a serpentine writhe gives an increased perspective of the variation of the motley heads. Every man must decide for himself, according to his taste and the shape of his garden.

Irises should be moved now, in June or July, after they have finished flowering, so this is the time to do it. They are a most generous grower, allowing themselves to be split up into dozens of roots or rhizomes from one root or rhizome which you may have bought at a high price a year or so ago. Take the side bits off the rhizome and plant them separately, and within a couple of years you will get a fresh clump for nothing. Cut off any diseased or squelchy bit of the original rhizome, and burn it.

I cannot, in this short article, give a list of the loveliest irises to grow—you must get a catalogue from an iris nurseryman. You will discover from this that many of the irises have come down in price. *Spindrift*, for example, has dropped from 12s. 6d. to 5s. and many of the older kinds, such as *Melchior*, *Ambassadeur*, and *Cinnabar* are now to be obtained at 2s. each.

Please remember also *Iris sibirica*. This slim and graceful iris will grow anywhere, either by the water side or in a border. It has the pleasant habit of sowing itself accidentally in odd corners and of appearing where we never thought to see it, and it always looks nice, wherever it comes up.

June 23, 1957

I salute the courage and enterprise of some people. Here is a well-known firm, Fison's, opening a sort of Inquiry Bureau in London, where perplexed and puzzled gardeners can apply for advice, either by letter or by telephone, Welbeck 5500, and get a reply to any horticultural problem from how to discover the pH constituent of their soil to the elimination of daisies in their lawns. You just write, or ring up, and get the answer.

It is a brave idea, and I wish it well. Frequently and gratefully in the future shall I dial Welbeck 5500 to inquire what climber will flourish over a pergola in a swamp, or what shrubs will give a flowering period for at least six months of the year and also look nice throughout the winter, or what can we plant please Miss Sackville-West round our front lawn which is nothing but a heap of clay and rubble

chucked out by the builders, and please Miss Sackville-West
could you tell us what we should do about the neighbours'
cats and our own sparrows and blue-tits that peck off all our
fruit buds, and please Miss Sackville-West could you tell us
about what to grow in a London garden with bad sour soil
and no sunlight ever reaching it. . . .

All these questions are now going to be resolved by the
Garden Centre, Fison House, 95, Wigmore Street, London,
W.1.

June 24, 1956

People who grow irises must have been pleased this year.
They came up in such profusion, after the sun-baking they
got in the summer of 1955.

The iris is one of the easiest plants to grow, and for this
reason is often asked to put up with much unreasonable ill-
treatment. Only too frequently is it stuffed away in some
shady corner, where it will loyally comply in producing a
few spikes, but put it in full sun and observe the difference.
It may even be given a sticky waterlogged soil, which it
much dislikes, but give it a serviceable well-drained soil,
and again observe the difference. It also likes lime, either
in the form of old mortar rubble or ground chalk; and a
handful of bonemeal to the square yard will not come amiss.

One great advantage of the iris is the rapidity with which
it increases. I know that some of the better varieties are
expensive to buy, but one single rhizome will triplicate or
quadruplicate itself within twelve months as inexorably as
any official form, but far more rewardingly. This is the time
of year to divide and replant irises. Dig up the clump,
which looks like a cluster of fat brown crayfish, and you will
find a number of white roots just beginning to grow. Cut
out the centre of the clump, which is the part that has
flowered, and retain only the younger side-bits. Replant
these, singly, one by one, without burying them under the

soil. This sounds easier than it is in practice, for you have to set them firmly in order to prevent them from getting loosened and wobbling about. It is one of those things that expert gardeners cheerfully advise one to do, and then go off leaving one wondering how to do it.

An old argument concerns the shortening of the leaves. Some people say you shouldn't; other people say you should. The people who say you should, contend that the newly-planted rhizome runs less risk of being loosened by wind when it has not got a tall fan of leaves to be blown over. I am on the side of the shorteners. I would not cut the leaf down to the base, of course I would not, but I cannot see that it does any harm to cut the leaves half way down, because the top-tips will die off anyhow and turn brown, so there can be no loss of green vegetable nutriment to the root at the bottom, that secret store whence astonishing flowers astonishingly arise.

June 26, 1955

Not nearly enough use is made of that airy flower, the modern columbine. Even our old native *Aquilegia vulgaris* has its charm. Who could resist anything nicknamed Granny's Bonnet or Doves-round-a-dish? I never have the heart to tear it out from wherever it has chosen to sow itself, though I know that it is little more than a weed and is a nuisance in that it hybridizes to the detriment of the choicer kinds. In fact, there are few flowers better disposed to hybridize amongst themselves, or, as one nurseryman puts it, 'their morals leave much to be desired.' In the case of the columbines, however, this is part of their attraction, for it means you may get chance seedlings of a colour you never anticipated.

Let me list their other advantages. They are perennial, which saves a lot of bother. They are hardy. They are light and graceful in a mixed bunch. They will put up with a certain amount of shade. They are easily grown from seed, and may be had in a surprising range of height and hue, from the tiny blue *alpina* whose inch of stature makes it suitable for rockeries, to the 3-ft. long-spurred hybrids in yellow, white, blue, mauve, pink, crimson-and-gold; and even, if you want something really out of the way, in green-and-brown. This last one is called *viridiflora*, and is about a foot high. I regret that I do not know where to obtain its seed; a plant from Mr. Stuart Boothman, Nightingale Nursery, Maidenhead, costs 2s., but should be a good investment, as it will set seed of its own accord for future increase.

For any lucky person with the space to spare, I could imagine a small enclosed garden or, say, a three-sided court-yard such as you often find in old farmhouses. If the court-yard happened to be paved with flagstones, so much the better, for, as I never tire of saying, plants love to get between the cracks and send their roots down into the cool reaches of the soil beneath, thus preserving themselves from the minor enemy of frost and from the major enemy of damp. It is just such a little walled garden or courtyard that I envisage, blowing with a coloration of columbines.

June 30, 1957

A shrub which has given me great delight over at least four weeks of flowering is *Abutilon vitifolium*, but before praising it let me list its drawbacks, always the more prudent method. First, it is not a plant for harsh climates. Given a sheltered angle between walls or hedges, it will survive a reasonable winter in the southern and, of course, the south-western counties, but would not like being planted in the open in some bleak spot of the Midlands or East Anglia. Second, it is not very long-lived, and may die abruptly, leaving a painful blank. Third—no, there seems no third objection to set against it, so now I can come on to the praise.

As its adjectival name suggests, it has a vine-like leaf, of a pale greenish-grey, thickly clothed in May and June with five-petalled flowers either of pale lavender, the colour of Parma violets, or a pure white with golden anthers. You must decide for yourselves which you prefer, the mauve or the white. Having a predilection for white flowers I gave my heart to the white, a ghostly apparition seen by moonlight. The flowers are rather like a single hollyhock, which is comprehensible since the abutilon belongs to the *malvaceae* or mallows, but it also suggests a resemblance to the tall Japanese anemone, if you can imagine a Japanese anemone deciding to turn itself into a shrub.

* * *

It will grow 10 ft. high or more, quite quickly; and although it has this unfortunate habit of suddenly dying, it can easily be kept going by its own seeds which it produces in the usual squandering quantities Nature thinks necessary. A few seeds sown in a pot should supply enough young plants to replace their grandmothers. Seeds may come true, but one has to take the chance of getting the mauve or the white form, always rather an exciting experiment to see what one is going to get.

Abutilon vitifolium comes from Chile and was first introduced into Ireland in 1836, so it has been quite a long time in our gardens. A lovely cool-looking shrub for the spring months or early summer, I would recommend it every time. I think it ought to be well placed, against a dark background if possible, say a dark hedge to show up the pallor of the silvery leaf and the flower. A great deal depends on the right placing of any plant, as I always try to emphasize in all these articles.*

* I must here add, for the benefit of any reader interested in *Abutilon vitifolium*, that someone has very kindly sent me some seedlings of a double or semi-double pink form he found growing in southern Spain. This should prove an acquisition, if it can be made to thrive in this country.

July

July 1, 1956

I HAVE written before now in this column about the great
bearded irises of June.

Might I now add a plea for the smaller irises, the
tinies? They, also, should be divided up and replanted just
now. You will find many of them in the nurseryman's catalogues under the name *pumila*; they are ideal for the rock-
garden, in a sunny, well-drained pocket.

Iris cristata is even smaller. Three inches high. It is sometimes called *lacustris*, meaning a lake-dweller and thus
indicating that it prefers a moist soil. It will do best in
semi-shade, in a mixture of sand and peat, and the same
remark applies to *Iris gracilipes*, with rush-like leaves. *Iris
graminea* is perhaps a plant for the connoisseur, not that it
is difficult to grow, but that it makes rather an untidy patch
of leaf and is of no showy garden value. Its value lies entirely
in picking for a very intimate sniff in a glass on one's own
writing-table or dressing-table. It smells of ripe apricots or
greengages. The flowers hide themselves beneath the leaves,
and you have to hunt for them, as you sometimes have to
hunt for a hidden quality in a human friend. So many
human beings take an immense amount of unnecessary
trouble to conceal their real selves inside a camouflage of
leaves.

And this reminds me of *Iris innominata*. Nothing could
be more secretive or anonymous than a plant refusing to
give itself a name. I believe that this exquisite little iris

comes from Oregon, in the north of the United States. Mrs. Anley, who knows more about irises than most people, calls it 'a lovely little iris, but not very easy.' I have found it very easy indeed, although I am no expert to compare with Mrs. Anley's experience and should hesitate to go counter to her judgment. All I can say is that it flourishes and flowers richly and generously in my garden, in its various colours of yellow, mauve and buff-brown, but the one thing it does resent is any attempt to divide or lift it. If it is happy, let it be.

I am well aware that this is a very amateurish article. I have tried to suggest only a few of the dwarf irises I grow for my pleasure. There are many others which I have not even mentioned: *Iris attica*, and the tiny *Iris mellita*, only 6 in. high. I haven't got this so I can't say much about it, except that it comes from the Balkans and likes as much sun as it can get. It is a very wide subject; and leaves me thinking how fortunate other countries are, in the wealth of irises that grow there native in the conditions that suit them. The sea-green *Iris persica*, for example, which shoots up through the stony deserts of Persia after the first spring rains. I have dug that up, and brought it home, but did it care for our island climate? No.

July 3, 1955

Lilacs (now called Syringa) have worried me for years past. I could not discover how to treat them right, and as I find that other people have been equally worried, I have been asking advice from two or three expert growers and hope that I may have obtained some useful hints to pass on.

The lilac grows grandly. It grows into a great tall tree-like shrub, if you allow it to grow without restraint, so tall that after a few years it over-tops our own heads by several yards, so high that we can neither pick the heavy panicle of flower, nor enjoy the scent as we wander round the garden. It is too high out of reach.

What are we going to do about it, to save it from becoming too tall and straggly?

I think I now know.

I need hardly say that all the seeding heads should be cut off at once, to save the plant from the effort of seeding itself, but in addition to this annual attention paid by the merest amateur with a bush or two of lilac in his garden, I would add this bit of advice. You should cut your lilacs hard back. Take them right back to a new leaf-bud, and encourage them to break out afresh. Cut out all dead and twiggy wood, opening the centre to receive as much air and light as possible. This is the time to perform these surgical operations, just after the flowering; take note to do it without delay. And if you have got any manure available, put it round your lilacs now; they need feeding; they will appreciate a rich mulch. If you haven't got organic manure, or compost, give them some handfuls of bonemeal or hoof-and-horn, pricking the top-spit lightly with a fork to give them the benefit of a loosened top-soil so that the rain can wash it in.

This treatment should do your lilacs good. It will make them bushy instead of straggly. I hope so. I must admit that the drastic pruning advocated alarms me; but I dare say that my advisers are right, and I am always disposed to accept the advice of people who know their own job better than I can ever pretend to know it.

July 7, 1957

During the now many years since I have been writing this weekly article for *The Observer* I must surely have recommended *Hoheria lyallii*. I can't think why people don't grow it more often, if they have a sheltered corner and want a tall 10-ft. shrub that flowers in that awkward time between late June and early July, smothered in white-and-gold flowers of the mallow family, to which the hollyhock also belongs, and sows itself in such profusion that you could have a whole forest of it if you had the leisure to prick out the seedlings and the space to replant them.

It really is a lovely thing, astonishing me every year with its profusion. I forget about it; and then there it is again with its flowers coming in their masses suggesting phila-delphus, for which it might easily be mistaken, but even more comely than any philadelphus, I think, thanks to the far prettier and paler leaf. A native of the South Island of New Zealand, it has the reputation of not being quite hardy in the colder parts of this country. That is why I said grow it in a sheltered corner. All I can tell you is that it has survived many frosty winters here in Kent (not so favour-able a climate as, say, Sussex, let alone the further western counties), including the dreadful ice-rain winter of 1946–47 and the cruel February of 1956, more recent in our memo-ries, and that seems a good enough recommendation or character-reference for giving so lovely a thing a chance.

It has other advantages. It doesn't dislike a limy soil, always an important consideration for people who garden on chalk and can't grow any of the lime-haters. It doesn't like rich feeding, which tends to make it produce leaf rather than flower. This means an economy in compost or organic manures or inorganic fertilizers which could be better ex-pended elsewhere. Bees love it. It is busy with bees, making their midsummer noise as you pass by.

There seems to be some confusion about what it should properly be called. I knew it first as *Plagianthus lyallii*, but now it has turned into *Hoheria lyallii* and I am content to accept it as that. So long as a shrub gives me so much pleasure I cannot mind or bother over-much about what the botanists decide to call it. I am no botanical expert; I just know, amateurishly, what looks nice in my garden and suggest what might look equally nice in yours.

July 8, 1956

Last year, I seem to remember, we said the roses had never been more generous of their giving, and this year we are saying the same again. We should be grateful for such repetitive munificence.

This year we should recognize a special gratitude. Something held the roses back. They never caught up with the irises that usually flower at the same time; and this meant that although the irises were not quite over, there was still a profusion of roses to come. Masses of bud still waiting to open, even after Midsummer Day.

I am not here thinking of the Hybrid Teas, well-groomed, well-taught, compliant, and as tidy as any lady of fashion. I can see their beauty and their usefulness, but it is the gipsy roses that take my heart. More primly, people now call them the shrub roses, which indeed is a right and proper name for a rose that is in fact a flowering shrub, but to me they are the gipsies of the rose-tribe. They resent restraint; they like to express themselves in all their vigour freely as the fancy takes them, free as the dog-rose in the hedgerows, I know they are not to everybody's taste, and I know that it isn't everybody who has room for them in a small garden, but all the same I love them much and would sacrifice much space to them.

I wonder how many people grow a particularly charming single pink rose, well adapted for tumbling over a low wall, called *Rosa sancta*, or the Holy Rose of Abyssinia? Its name alone would justify its inclusion, and so would its history, for historically it is one of the oldest known roses and may well be the subject of a Minoan fresco at Cnossos in Crete. It has also been found woven into garlands in Egyptian tombs, so what more could any rose ask from its ancestry? It is not easy to come by, and I notice that Mr. Bertram Park does not include it in his indispensable new *Guide to Roses* (Collins, 25s.). A vice-president of the National Rose

Society and editor of the *Rose Annual*, Mr. Park's name is familiar to rosarians, and I fancy that no rose-grower, whether on a small or a large scale, will wish to be without this extremely useful and compendious volume.

Even though Mr. Park may disdain the Holy Rose, Messrs. Edwin Murrell don't. Their address will be found on page 197 of this book.

July 10, 1955

I have always been torn in half between a mistrust of gadgets and a desire to experiment with them. Sundries Avenue at the Chelsea Show has a disastrous attraction for me as for the other 40,000 Fellows of the R.H.S. and for the further 400,000 members of the gardening public crowding through the turnstiles on the following days. We all hope, pathetically and optimistically, to discover something which will lighten our toil, and how seldom do we find it. We always come back in the end to the proven tools: the sharp fork, the blunt hoe, the solid old spade and its small brother the trowel; all tools that Man has evolved to his use since he first began to cultivate his patch of ground in the Dark Ages.

Yet it would be both stupid and obstructive to deny the uses of some modern inventions. There was a time, not so very long ago, when grass had to be scythed by hand. Where are the scythesmen now? Few countrymen have the skill, or the patience, or the desire, to lay those rhythmical swathes hour by hour from the dews of morning when long grass cuts easiest and best, to the hot high sun of midday, and then through the extended heat of afternoon to the eventual cool of evening when the scythe is hitched up for the night in its resting-place in the barn or the tool-shed.

These days have gone. We now have a less picturesque but far speedier substitute for the old man with his scythe. It cost £48 10s. to buy; a lot of money, but it has earned its keep over and over again in the three years we have had it.*

One of its advantages is that it carries a little wooden platform or shield to cover its revolving blade, thus rendering it impossible for even the most reckless jobbing gardener to slice a promising plant to a stub 2 in. from the ground. Many are the flowering trees and shrubs I lost in the past, when they were young and small and tender, and got cut down by rough treatment among the orchard grass. Now the wooden shield just bumps softly against the stem and comes to a stop.

Then, to come down to a humbler, less mechanical form of gadget, the sort of gadget that will appeal to elderly gardeners such as myself, unable to stoop nimbly or to kneel with any pleasure or comfort as we did in our younger days, may I recommend a thing I turned my nose up at, rather contemptuously, as an amateurish thing to be despised by any true gardener? I am now a convert to it and could not be without it. It is the most ingenious kind of little stool; you can turn it either way up, to different heights, either to sit on or to kneel on, or even to stand on if you wish to reach up to an overhanging branch. It is quite light to carry about, although it is solid in its construction, being made of some kind of tubular metal.

This is called the Easy Kneeler, made by Messrs. Woodman, Pinner, Middlesex.

July 14, 1957

I know I have written about ixias in this column before now. I hate repeating myself, and try not to, but it was a long time ago, in 1952, so perhaps a reminder may come usefully, now that the autumn catalogues are getting smeared with jam and honey on the breakfast table every morning.

---

* It is called the Hayter Rotary Scythe and we got it from Hayters (Sales) Ltd., 14 Spellbrook Lane, Bishop's Stortford.

Ixias, or corn lilies, are natives of South Africa, and thus demand a well-drained gritty soil in the warmest place we can provide, at the foot of a south wall, in just such a place as you would set Iris *stylosa* (*unguicularis*) starved and baked to flower at its best. A raised bed would be ideal for ixias, where you could probably keep them going for years and years, but who amongst us has the time or the labour to construct a raised bed? On the whole I have found the ixias reasonably reliable, even in an ordinary flat bed. It is true that they diminish instead of increasing with the years, but they are so cheap at 2s. a dozen mixed, or 2s. 3d. to 2s. 6d. for named varieties, that a dozen or so can be added each year to replenish the stock.

They are also so graceful, somewhat resembling freesias, on their wiry stems, and so pretty in their range of odd colourings, rose-pink, straw, yellow, white, coppery, and so good for picking, that a couple of dozen at least ought to be in every garden.

Loveliest of all, perhaps, is *Ixia viridiflora*, sea-green with a black eye, a treasure for connoisseurs but becoming so rare as to be difficult to obtain. When I was recently in Cape Town, I thought my chance had come to buy dozens of its bulbs, but could get only a dozen. It appears that the area of its incidence is fiercely and legally protected, but has already been much depleted. If any nursery-man lists it, I shall be glad to hear from him.*

Botanically related to the ixias, since they both belong to the iris family, are the *sparaxis*. The best known is the Wand-flower, *sparaxis pulcherrima*, now called *Dierama pulcherrima*, a graceful but rather untidy thing for which I know I ought to, but cannot, entertain a deep affection.

---

* This appeal produced several sources of supply: Messrs. Kelway, Langport, Somerset; D. and W. Pigott, Furze Hill Nursery, Wimborne, Dorset; M. K. Kooper, Ferndown, Dorset.

It may look right in the suitable setting of a water-side, and I will agree that its constantly moving stems blown by a breeze across the water have a windy wandy charm and quality all of their own. All the same, I prefer the true sparaxis one grows in the same way as an ixia, that is to say in a warm south-facing bed under a wall, or in a pan under glass for early flowering, or in the rock-garden, where it should live happily for years, given the sharp drainage all these South Africans need.

I have kept a pan of sparaxis for years, cruelly neglected, but coming up and flowering gallantly every spring. There is a particularly showy one amongst them, which I think must be *Excelsior*, a very brilliant dark red with a yellow eye and black splotches.

July 15, 1956

If you already grow daphnes in your garden, this is the time to watch the ripening seeds unless you want the birds to take them. There is every advantage in raising your own young stock from seed. Daphnes are not long-lived, and after a few years have a distressing habit of dying suddenly for no apparent reason, so it is well to have some young plants coming along. These young replacements should be grown from seed in pots, one seed to a pot. Daphnes hate being disturbed, but if you tip them out of a pot, roots and all, they scarcely notice what you are doing to them and grow happily away. They may also be sown straight into the ground where they are intended to remain. One can raise such a quantity from seed, that one can afford the extravagance of sticking them into likely and unlikely places, experimenting to find out where they will thrive, as one could not do if one bought them for big shillings from a nursery.

Daphne mezereum is probably the most familiar. It seems to thrive in cottage gardens, with the same inverted snobbishness exhibited by the Madonna lily. Opinions differ very much as to whether it approves of a peaty soil or of something sharper and more stony; one has even heard of it growing in gravel. By nature it would appear to be a woodlander, yet some authorities tell us to place it in full sun, so it is not without reason that I suggest experimenting with it in different situations. If you plant it in full sun, however, it does seem to appreciate some flat stones over its roots to keep them cool. The mezereon flowers in early spring on leafless branches, very sweet scented and purplish-pink in colour; there is also a white variety, very beautiful, and possibly more reliable. You can tell by the fruits which kind you are collecting, for the type has red fruits and the white variety yellow.

Daphne retusa is a much stockier little shrub, with a rounded top, seldom exceeding 3 ft. in height, sometimes confused with *Daphne tangutica*, but preferable, I think, because of its more compact growth. I like it greatly. It is far hardier than the intensely fragrant *Daphne odora*, which really demands protection or a greenhouse, although an outdoor plant of mine came safely through 20 degrees of frost last winter. A little hedge of *Daphne retusa*, bordering a path, would be amusing, especially if it followed the line of some steps and ended on an eminence in the rock-garden, perched like an ibex amongst some boulders. I fancy that it is one of the easiest of the daphnes, far easier than the capricious *cneorum*, the envy of every rock-gardener who has failed to grow it successfully. Those who fail should try its child, known as *Daphne Somerset*.

July 17, 1955

There are few more decorative climbers for mid-summer than the great hybrid clematis, but their distressing habit of suddenly collapsing from the fungus disease most descriptively known as *wilt*, when at the height of their beauty, discourages many people from planting them. This disease is especially likely to occur when the clematis has been grafted, and has not been grown, as it should be, on its own roots. There is, however, a shrubby or herbaceous kind of clematis which does not appear to be so liable to wilt, and which is well worth considering as an ornament to any border.

It is not so often seen as the climbers, and it cannot claim to be so showy, but it has its attraction and its uses. *Clematis recta* is the earliest to flower, usually in June, making a dense bush from 4 to 6 ft. in height, a mass of starry white clusters, faintly scented, borne on very straight stems; it comes easily from seed. *C. heracleifolia*, which means having leaves like cow-parsley, is blue in flower, and so is its hybrid *C. jouiniana*, with its varieties *campanile* and *Cote d'Azur*; these will grow 3 to 5 ft. by July or August, their flowering season. They can be grown from seed or from cuttings or root division.

C. integrifolia has been known in this country ever since 1596. It seldom grows taller than 2 ft., so can be used to advantage in the rockery as well as in the front of a bed or border, in fact it really looks its best among stones where it will not require any staking, but may be allowed to trail. For the same reason it makes a graceful contribution to a dry wall, if you are lucky enough to possess such a thing. The blue form, to my thinking, is preferable to the white, but some variation must be expected. It can be grown from seed, which reminds me to remark how very obligingly most clematis lend themselves to this method of propagation, as also to cuttings and to layering. The seed may be collected from the silvery heads of all such early flowerers as *C. macropetala* and sown as soon as ripe; the large summer varieties will of course not ripen until much later on, so sowing is best deferred until the following spring. Cuttings should be taken in August, and they do not seem to mind whether you take them just below a node or between two nodes; either way is equally successful, if you press them very firmly into a potful of the sandy compost usual for any cutting, and water them in.

Layering is perhaps more likely to appeal to the professional gardener, though anybody who is accustomed to layering pinks and carnations will find no difficulty in pursuing the same method. Whichever you elect to do, you will at least be certain of having your clematis growing on its own roots, which means no suckers and a greater resistance to the dreaded wilt.

July 21, 1957

The floribunda roses are very much in the news just now, and small wonder, for the choice is becoming so varied, their colourings so brilliant, their flowering period so prolonged, their value as cut flowers so remarkable, and their vigour so satisfactory. There is nothing to be said against them, and everything to be said in their favour, so I suppose it will provoke cries of indignation if I prophesy that within a very few years the more fastidious gardener will come to regard them with as much contempt as he now regards Dorothy Perkins, American Pillar, and many members of the Poulsen clan. Already the floribundas are beginning to invade municipal gardens and road roundabouts, and although I am no advocate of gardening snobbishness, if a plant is beautiful in itself, I have a suspicion that the floribundas will not survive the test of too widespread a ubiquity.

Meanwhile there is no denying that they are very useful. I like the truly sumptuous red of *Frensham*, *Dusky Maiden*, *Donald Prior*, and *Moulin Rouge*. I like the little salmon-coloured *Fashion*, and the freakish joke of *Masquerade* in its three different colours like a flag. I like all the *Pinocchios*: pink, white, or yellow, and the one called *Lavender* which is not lavender at all but brown, like a bruise, not everybody's taste, I know: 'What, that dirty-looking thing?' I like *Rosemary Rose*, which nobody could call dirty for it is of a carmine to make you blink, and thus rather difficult to place with other colours in the garden, but what a flower for a vase. The hideously named *August Seebauer* does not seem to be very well known, but is a splendid rose with huge pink double flowers; *Ma Perkins* also seems an unfortunate name for a rose but is deservedly popular; *Jiminy Cricket* on the other hand is rather an engaging name for a recent introduction, 1954, a coppery-orange, bushy and very free flowering.

It is good to get these orange colourings, for the flaming old *Austrian Copper* was seldom a vigorous doer, and there are also some fine yellows among the floribundas: *Sandringham*, which makes a tall plant if not hard-pruned, and *Sunny Maid*, another tall grower. The tall floribundas are said to make attractive hedges; and although I can imagine that they would not be solid enough for a boundary hedge, I can quite see that they would be extremely merry as a division between two parts of the garden. One rosarian suggests a double hedge, with floribundas in front and hybrid musks behind. For anyone able to afford the space (and the plants) this should prove a profitable idea, with continuous bloom throughout the summer. The musks would supply the scent the floribundas lack.

July 22, 1956

Rumours and more than rumours have reached Britain of a strange new strawberry which is a climber. In German the name for strawberry is Erdbeeren, meaning earth-berry, fruiting tight to the earth, but as the Germans rightly remark the name will be no longer applicable to this new object, which will grow to a height of 6 ft. and may be trained against a trellis; in fact, they already call it the espalier strawberry. Very pretty and unusual, with the bright red berries hanging in clusters, I should say, judging by a photograph I have seen in a German paper. The fruit is said to be of a good flavour, full-sized, and resembling *St. Claude* in its conical shape and brilliant colour. *St. Claude* is perhaps not very well known as yet, but a fine future is predicted for it as a heavy and perpetual cropper.

Unfortunately the rumours of the climbing strawberry have not been followed into Britain by any samples of the plant itself. It has travelled from Elmshorn in Schleswig-Holstein into France, where it is now called *Truffaut-Prodige* and is very jealously guarded by its nurseryman-owner. Not a single plant is for export. If you happen to live in France and want to grow it in your own French garden and buy a plant from him, you have to promise on oath that you will not bring it out of France. Honour thus forbids me to supply his address to any potential sponge-bag smuggler crossing the Channel. One has one's principles, even in these days.

I do hope, however, that this remarkable development of the climbing strawberry will soon be released on to our island market, and I thought it might be of interest to my readers to know about it in advance, so that they can put their names down on the queue for the orders that are sure to pour in. *

To turn to a very different subject. Weeds and pests are always a nuisance and a worry. You can now obtain, free of charge, a list of approved products from the Ministry of Agriculture, Fisheries and Food, Soho Square, London. I feel sure that this hint will prove useful to people who have perhaps not discovered the paternal interest taken by a Government Office in the troubles of us poor gardeners.

July 24, 1955

It is a sad moment when the first phlox appears. It is the amber light indicating the end of the great burst of early summer and suggesting that we must now start looking

* See, however, p.52, and illustration opposite p.48. March 31, 1957.

forward to autumn. Not that I have any objection to autumn as a season, full of its own beauty; but I just cannot bear to see another summer go, and I recoil from what the first hint of autumn means.

Still, one must make up one's mind to it, and be philosophical, and make the best of what is left to us. The herbaceous phlox will do much to comfort us in the late summer and early autumn months. It does give a sumptuous glowing show, especially if you can plant it in a half-shady bed where its colours will curiously change with the sinking sun and will deepen with twilight into colours you never thought it possessed.

I feel sure that this is the way to grow phlox: in a cool, north-aspect border, all to themselves, not mixed up with other things in a hot sunny border.

They look better in isolation, closely packed; and a rather damp soil and lots of rich feeding. This means organic manure from the cowshed or pigsty if you can get it; or the indispensable bonemeal or hoof-and-horn from the shop if you can't. A mulch of peat or compost likewise provides encouragement. Anything that will keep the roots cool and will give them something to eat.

The chief enemy of the herbaceous phlox, *P. decussata*, is the small but wicked eel-worm. This is not the same brand as attacks potatoes and the bulbs of narcissus. The phlox specializes in a form of eel-worm which affects the stem and not the root. The leaves curl up and the whole plant begins to look unmistakably miserable. There is no cure unless you are prepared to use a rather dangerous remedy called *parathion*. If you are not prepared to do this, and I really wouldn't advise it for the amateur gardener, the only alternative is to cut down the infested stems *now*, and take root cuttings from your plants next April when they begin to shoot up. Thus you will get a healthy stock, free from eel-worm, that tiny destructive organism which,

I suppose, must have its life, even as we must all have our lives, predatory, competitive, and preying on our fellow-beings even though we would prefer it not to find its nourishment on the phlox we have carefully arranged to give some colour to our late-summer and early-autumn garden.

July 28, 1957

Faithful to the principle that autumn catalogues will shortly be arriving, I propose to devote the next few Sundays to notes on some roses less frequently grown than the hybrid teas, climbers, ramblers, and other popular kinds. Useful though they undeniably are, some people like to get away from the orthodox and try something different. It is for those people that I write these articles. *

A rose which always catches the eye of visitors to my garden is an old Hybrid perpetual (1867) called *Baron Giraud de l'Ain*. This is a dark red rose with crinkly petals edged in white. I am not very well versed in dress-making terms, but I am given to understand that this sort of edging is called picot in English and by the French *engrêlure*, not to be confused with *engelures*, meaning chilblains. This picot-edged rose is, in my experience, a far stronger grower than the almost indistinguishable *Roger Lambelin* (1890): Giraud seems to be blessed with a better constitution than his younger brother Roger.

Then there is the green rose. Admittedly this is a freak, and you may not like it. I don't like it very much myself; but I have a sentimental feeling for it because it grew in my old home when I was a child and one preserves a

* These notes will be found under the dates August 4, 11, 18, 25, and September 1 and 8, 1957.

There are two other articles about roses, on pp. 156 and 160, October 2, and October 9, 1955.

People often ask me where to get these roses. I refer them to Messrs. Edwin Murrell, whose address will be found on p. 197.

sentimental feeling for everything one knew as a child before
the cares and worries of adult life came upon one. The
green rose is called *Rosa chinensis viridiflora*. It makes no
show in the garden, but is surprisingly decorative in a vase
for picking.

One could wish only that it lived up to its name and was
truly green, not tinged with brown. A jade green rose
would be something worth having, but even the lovers of
the so-called green rose must confess that its flowers are a
bit smudgy. Either you love it, or you have no use for it;
it all depends on what you feel.

The rose called *Turkestanica*, or *Tipo ideale*, or *chinensis
mutabilis* is likely to please anybody with a freakish taste.
Well grown, it makes a big bush apparently smothered in
several sorts of butterflies: pink, yellow and cream. It will
flower all through the summer, especially if you can give
it a sunny, sheltered corner. I do recommend this, if you
don't already know it. It is a china with a fairly long history,
and has had the honour of being drawn by Redouté.

July 29, 1956

I have been much struck this month by the beauty of the
philadelphus. We used to call it syringa, with Mock Orange
as its English name, but philadelphus seems to suit it nicely,
meaning brotherly or sisterly love in Greek, suggesting a
purity of love distinct from any sexual passion.

Yet the thing is bridal. It makes huge bushes of the
purest white. The love of siblings may be all very well,
but it is a truly nuptial thing, an epithalamium of a poem
for young lovers.

I saw it foaming about in two famous gardens I recently
went to in Gloucestershire. I saw it also in all the cottage
gardens of that incomparable Cotswold country. It was
everywhere; all over the place. I scolded myself for not
having planted philadelphus in masses when I first started

to make my garden. Had I done so years ago, I should have had huge bushes by now, but it is never too late.

I have got the dear old *Philadelphus coronarius*, that sweet-scented bush that takes one straight back to one's childhood. Three hundred years ago, Gerard the herbalist wrote that he had cut some flowers of this old plant, and laid them in his chamber, but found them of so un-acquainted a savour that he could not take rest until he had cast them out. This can mean only that he found the scent too strong. What I hadn't realized was that some of the later flowering sorts were almost equally generous of their scent. Now I know better. The little *microphyllus* may not be very showy but smells delicious in its small white flowers. *Lemoinei erecturus* is also sweet-scented. *Belle Etoile* isn't; or at any rate I can't detect any scent in it. Perhaps that is the fault of my nose; anyhow it is so magnificent a shrub that we all ought to grow it.

The philadelphus family is so complicated that it is diffi-cult to distinguish between them. They hybridize so freely amongst themselves that scarcely anybody knows now which are species or which are hybrids. Do we have to worry about this? Should we not rather plant as many as we can secure, this autumn, in the anticipation of great white bushes a few years hence?

July 31, 1955

For the first time, this year, urged and prodded by a friend of mine whose name as a seedsman is famous throughout this country, I got a packet of seed called *Mesem-bryanthemum criniflorum*, less alarmingly named the Livingstone Daisy. He coaxed me into ordering that one little seed-packet, and I am now glad that I took his advice. It is just beginning to open its starry flowers, and, my good-ness, how pretty it promises to be. It startles with its colour as I see it in the early morning when the dew still lays its grey veils over the turf, and there at the end of the lawn in the distance comes a bright, brilliant little thing, making me blink my eyes to see what it can be.

I know what it is, because I planted it. I wasn't sure what it was going to look like, but am now pleased with what it is doing for me. Very much pleased indeed. It is making a mat of low-growing, rather ugly leaf, which for some reason looks as though somebody had been trampling on it, a squashed-down-looking leaf, very plain and somewhat succulent, but as the sun rises higher it quickly disappears beneath the crowds of bright faces, each about the size of a half-crown, in a kaleidoscope of magenta, pink, yellow, apricot, deep rose, buff, and a light golden straw. Of course, they will close up again when the sun leaves them, but meanwhile you could not have a prettier harlequin.

Unfortunately it is only half-hardy, so must be raised from seed under glass in March, pricked off into seed boxes, and planted out at the end of May or beginning of June. If this involves too much trouble, or if no glass is available, you could sow it out of doors in May, when naturally it would flower later. Being a desert plant (South Africa) it likes the sharpest possible drainage and a poor soil, so do not waste a good enriched border which would be the delight of greedier things. I imagine that it would revel in the top of a dry wall, in the sort of situation where one often sees the yellow sedum growing wild in stone-wall country, and here I would not be surprised to find it naturalizing itself in warm cracks and reappearing of its own accord after the winter.

Another use to which it can be put is to provide colour in a rock garden, often rather drab after the Alpines and small spring things have gone. Remember always that it must have a place in the sun, or it will remain shut and sulky, a spoilt child.

August

August 4, 1957

WHATEVER differences of opinion we may hold about roses, and whether our taste inclines to the hybrid teas, or to the ramblers or to the old shrub roses, there is one thing on which we are all in agreement: it is an advantage for a rose to smell like a rose. The accusation is often brought against what people loosely call 'modern roses' that they have lost their scent, an accusation sometimes but not always justified. *Charles Mallerin,* for instance, that magnificent black-red hybrid tea, dates back only ten years and is as rich in scent as it is in colour. I recall also, and still grow, a huge pink climber called *Colcestria* which won the competition for the best-scented rose somewhere back in the 1920's; I cannot find it listed in any catalogue now, which seems a pity as it is not only powerfully scented but is what nurserymen describe as 'vig.' I must try to propagate it.

There are roses which are 'fast of their scent,' requiring to be held to the nose, and others which generously spread themselves upon the summer air. Of these, I would signal three in particular: *rosa rugosa alba* and *rugosa blanc double de Coubert,* and the hybrid musk *Penelope.* These all make big bushes, and should be placed near a corner where you frequently pass. They all have the merit of continuous flowering, and *rugosa alba* produces bright red hips in autumn, like little round apples amongst the yellowing leaves, adding to its attraction, interest and charm.

The rugosa hybrid, *Parfum de l'Hay*, has the reputation of being one of the most strongly scented of all roses. Unfortunately its constitution is not as strong as its scent. Perhaps light soils don't suit it. Its companion, *Roseraie de l'Hay*, might do better, and smells nearly as good. Neither of them makes a big bush, so would be suitable for a small garden.

Souvenir du Docteur Jamain is an old hybrid perpetual which I am rather proud of having rescued from extinction. I found him growing against the office wall of an old nursery. No one knew what he was; no one seemed to care; no one knew his name; no one had troubled to propagate him. Could I dig him up, I asked? Well, if you like to risk it, they said, shrugging their shoulders; it's a very old plant, with a woody stiff root. I risked it; *Docteur Jamain* survived his removal; and now has a flourishing progeny in my garden and also on the market of certain rosarians to whom I gave him. *Docteur Jamain* is a deep red, not very large flowers, but so sweetly and sentimentally scented. Some writers would call it nostalgically scented, meaning everything that burying one's nose into the heart of a rose meant in one's childhood, or in one's adolescence when one first discovered poetry, or the first time one fell in love.

I think *Docteur Jamain* should not be planted in too sunny a place. He burns. A south-west aspect suits him better than full south.

August 5, 1956

If you have always acquired the habit of always carrying a pencil and note-book, this is a good time to jot down some effects of light on a summer evening. The westering sun strikes through petals, making them look as though they were lit from within, not from without, and makes a picture unsuspected in the glare of noon when the sun stands high overhead.

This bright thought suggested itself to me as I observed a group of *Alstroemeria ligtu hybrids*, coral-pink and aureate, glowing in front of the towering plumes of *Bocconia cordata*, the Plume poppy, which again was backed by that small-flowered *Clematis kermesina* of a rich wine-red, climbing the wall behind it. The sun caught them all; and, looking at them, I thought this is the hour to see them, and this is the way to garden, putting everything in the place where it will catch the maximum of beauty that sunlight or evening light can give.

It is of course obvious that one should set plants designed for autumn-colour in a place where the sun will strike them. Everybody knows that. Maples and so on. But I do suggest to you that during this August holiday you might walk round your garden and notice the variation of light in our latening summer months, and record in a note-book the things you have observed. One says too easily, Oh, I shall remember that! and then time passes and one no longer remembers, and one tries to think back to that August evening when one knew there was something one intended to remember, but the vision had gone, and next year has come, and no record remains unless you have carried a pencil and a note-book always in your pocket.

August 7, 1955

One of the nicest things about gardening is the sudden surprise we may get when something that we arranged years ago comes into its own and is at last doing what we had intended it to do. We must admit that dusk is probably the kindest hour, lengthening the shadows, intensifying the colours, and obliterating the weeds, but nevertheless, I was not disappointed in the glare of the following morning by the great golden group I had observed in the after glow of a lingering sunset.

It was a group composed of ordinary, easy things, and

it was simply their collusion in flowering all together at the same time that made them so effective. In the foreground was a rounded shrub of cinquefoil, *Potentilla fruticosa*, with silvery leaves spattered by lemon-yellow flowers. Behind this arose the taller, flat-headed yellow yarrow, *Achillea eupatorium*, and then behind that the feathery meadow-rue, *Thalictrum glaucum*, a fluffy, saffron version of the brush we used to push up lamp-glasses before we had electric light. A few pale evening primroses had poked their untidy way upwards through a huge bush of the truly aureate St. John's Wort, *Hypericum patulum forrestii*, already massing the varnished buttercup of its half-crown-sized flower, and many buds coming on in promise. All this was good enough, but towering above the lot came the dripping glory of a great Mount Etna broom, *Genista ætnensis*, 10 ft. high, an arrested fountain of molten gold.

Now all these are easy-going plants, within the scope of every purse and experience or lack of experience, and if anybody had the space requisite to repeat this grouping in some lost corner where the sunset strikes, I think he would be pleased. Since one is never satisfied, however, I started making mental notes for improvement. The Hidcote variety of the St. John's Wort, for instance, is a finer thing than the type introduced by Forrest from China. Why hadn't I planted the Hidcote hypericum in the first instance? One should always plant the best, but one is ignorant to start with, and it takes years of floundering before one learns. And why had I not sent up some rockets of the giant mullein, *Verbascum olympicum*, to match the suspended fireworks of the Mount Etna broom? Why, indeed? I hope next year to repair my half-misspent time, but meanwhile my golden group gives me more pleasure than all the nuggets in the cellars of the Bank of England.

August 12, 1956

The big clematis hybrids make an imperial show in July and August, but are distressingly liable to the disease called wilt. They disappoint over and over again, collapsing overnight from the peak of their best to a misery of prostration, when there is nothing for it except to cut them down to the ground and hope that they may spring up again next year.

It is said that plants grown on their own roots do not suffer so badly from this fungoid disease for which no preventive or curative remedy has so far been found, and it is said also that dwellers on a limestone soil are far less troubled. All I can say is that my few big own-root clematis let me down as badly as the worst of false friends, and that I really cannot transfer my abode to Cumberland or Westmorland in order to please them.

It seems simpler to grow the kinds that are apparently immune.

I have found the species *C. viticella*, the Vine Bower, far less liable to wilt, and am glad to read that Ernest Markham shared my opinion. Mr. Markham was William Robinson's head gardener at Gravetye, where they made such grandly imaginative use of clematis, and where a chance seedling of the lavender-coloured *C. macropetala* turned up pink and was given the name *C. macropetala var. markhamii* in honour of a great gardener's great head-gardener.

*   *   *

Now to be practical. This month of August is the time to take cuttings. They root very readily, especially if taken between the nodes. This may sound odd, because as a rule one takes cuttings below a node, leaf-joint, or eye; but for some reason which I don't pretend to understand, the clematis prefers an inter-nodal cutting, half-way between one node and the next. It looks most unconvincing, but it does work. Try it.

Try also growing clematis from seed. Save your own seed from those flossy silky heads like a tiny grey turban of feather with a black little spot which is the seed. Germination should approach 100 per cent. The same applies to the herbaceous clematis, less often seen than the climbing sorts, although at least one of them, *C. integrifolia*, has been known in this country since 1596. About 2 ft. high, it is described as being of a velvety grey colour with a darker blue on the reverse. *C. recta*, another herbaceous plant, is taller, and in June is a mass of small white flowers, very effective, very useful.

August 11, 1957

To continue on the subject of roses I will now write about *Rosa alba*. This sounds as though it were invariably a white rose. Make no mistake. The adjective is misleading. Although it is true that *Rosa alba semi-plena* may have been the White Rose of York, and *alba maxima* the Great Double White or Jacobite rose, the alba roses include many forms which are not white but pink. The old *Maiden's Blush* of cottage gardens is an alba; the French called it *Cuisse de nymphe*, and when it appeared in an even rosier variant they called it *Cuisse de nymphe émue*. We, in our Puritanical England, acknowledge no truck with the thighs of nymphs, however emotional, so under the name of Maiden's Blush it remains, and a very pretty and innocent-looking pink and white débutante she is.

There are other alba roses which make my delight. Sometimes I think that *alba celestial* is one of the loveliest shrubs one could ever wish to contemplate, with its shell-pink flowers amongst its grey-green leaves. Then I look up into the tall bush of *Queen of Denmark* and think that she is possibly even more lovely, in a deeper pink than *alba celes-*

tial, with a quartered flower looking as though someone had taken a spoon and stirred it round, as a child might stir a bowl of strawberries and cream.

Mr. Edward Bunyard, who did so much to restore the historical roses to favour and circulation, was of the opinion that the albas were very useful in many unusual ways. They would tolerate difficult situations, thriving in soil penetrated by the roots of trees (he instances woodland walks); he claimed that they were resistant to mildew; and added that they could either be pruned or left unpruned, according to the taste of the grower, the space available, and the time that could be devoted to them. Mr. Graham Thomas, whose book *The Old Shrub Roses* I am constantly recommending, goes even further. According to him, they are resistant to all diseases; enjoy such vigour and longevity as to survive neglect for a hundred years; will grow in damp, cold, north-country gardens; and can successfully be planted against a north wall. Unlike Mr. Bunyard, however, he recommends that they should be closely pruned, in December or January, leaving the long shoots at one-third of their length, so between these two authorities we can take our choice and make our own experiments as to pruning.

August 14, 1955

The old, shrubby roses have long since spent their annual passion. They flowered this summer as they have never been seen to flower before, with a generosity that puzzled their growers. We all thought that the sunless summer of 1954 would fail to ripen any wood, and that all growth would go soft. On the contrary, the roses went wild in exuberance; I wonder they did not flower themselves to death. Never have I witnessed such a floraison as during this past June.

People are starting more and more to grow the old roses. It is a revival of the Victorian age, before we got the Hybrid Teas, so slick and perfectly shapely and sophisticated, and so very far removed from the sentimental appeal of that period now that we see it in perspective. True, most of the old Gallicas, Damasks, Centifolias and their many lovely fragrant companions suffer from one paramount drawback: they have only one flowering season in the year. This means that unless you can afford to devote a separate region to them, or are content with a few odd bushes here and there, in some lost corner where it will not matter having a green leafy bush instead of a bedizened voluptuous scented bush throughout most of the summer, the shrub roses are not for you. An exception must be made for the hybrid musks, which flower more or less continuously; and also for some of the rugosa group, so sweet-scented and so resistant to black-spot, mildew, and green-fly.

August 18, 1957

If you were born with a romantic nature, all roses must be crammed with romance, and if a particular rose originated on an island the romance must be doubled, for an island is romantic in itself.

The island I refer to lies off the south-east coast of Africa, near Mauritius. It used to be called the Ile Bourbon, now called Réunion. The inhabitants of this small island had the pleasing habit of using roses for their hedges: only two kinds, the Damask rose and the China rose. These two married in secret; and one day, in 1817, the curator of the botanic garden on the Ile Bourbon noticed a seedling he transplanted and grew on, a solitary little bastard which has fathered or mothered the whole race we now call the Bourbon roses.

It is curious to find Mr. Edward Bunyard writing in 1936 in his book *Old Garden Roses* that the Bourbon roses 'are now almost forgotten,' and listing only four as being 'still obtainable.' (*Hermosa, Bourbon Queen, Louise Odier,* and *Mme Pierre Oger.*) He does not even mention *Zéphyrine Drouhin,* the rose which so far back as 1868 decided to

discard armaments and has been known as the Thornless
rose ever since. This shows how taste has changed within
the last twenty years, for it is now possible to obtain at least
two dozen different varieties.

Far from being forgotten, now that the shrub roses have
returned to favour, *Rosa bourboniana* includes some of the
most desirable. Their scent alone makes one realize the
extent to which they have inherited that quality from their
damask parent; one has only to think of *Mme Isaac Péreire*
and *Mme Pierre Oger*, admittedly two of the most fragrant
roses in cultivation. We all have our scented favourites; and
someone is bound to say, 'What about *Parfum de l'Hay?*,'
but I must still support the claims of these two ladies in the
Bourbon group.

The cross has resulted in an oddly varied lot. There is
Coupe de Hebé, 1840, which you might easily mistake for a
centifolia or cabbage rose; and if you like the striped roses
there are *Honorine de Brabant* and *Commandant Beau-
paire*, 1874, pink and white like *Rosa mundi*, but not, I
contend, as good as that ancient Rose of the World. Among
the more recent crosses, *Zigeuner Knabe*, 1909, makes the
most swagger boastful bush you could set at any corner: a
reddish purple, it looks more like a Cardinal fully robed,
about to set off in procession, than like the *Gypsy Boy* we
call it in English.

August 19, 1956

Catalogues stream in by every post, bewildering in their
temptations. Everything sounds so desirable, and so easy to
grow. One has visions, like an opium dream of the Hanging
Gardens of Babylon. One knows quite well that one's own
garden is not like that at all, and never will be, but still how
hard it is to resist. Only 7s. 6d., we say; and then in a couple
of years' time we will have a great foaming bush or towering
tree; and so, recklessly, we order.

There are a few shrubs I should like to see on everybody's list, apart from the obvious ones. Starting with the earlier months of the year, the single-flowered *Kerria japonica* is much prettier than the double-flowered Kerria so often seen in old gardens. The single-flowered makes a bush apparently smothered in yellow butterflies, and has the advantage of putting up with quite a lot of shade, even under a north wall.

Later on two pink shrubs are very useful in a sunny border. *Kolkwitzia amabilis*, in May and June, and *Indigofera potanini*, in July and August, always attract attention and admiration. So does *Hoheria lyalli*, in late July, deceiving most people into thinking it is a philadelphus. Then in August, that difficult month, *Hibiscus syriacus*, a shrubby relation of the hollyhock or mallow, fills many an awkward empty gap. I like especially the white form with purple blotch at the base, reminiscent of a Victorian chintz, and, moreover, it seems to give more generously of its flowers than the blue and the red varieties.

None of these shrubs should be difficult to grow, or to obtain from any good nurseryman.

And if, finally, you want something to give colour throughout many months, especially in autumn, get *Rhus cotinus foliis purpureis, Notcutt's variety*. I apologize for this formidable name, but it is the only way in which I can define the best form of the sumptuous bush, which I would much rather call by its other name of Venetian Sumach. Venetian suggests all the brocades and velvets of Titian and Paolo Veronese, and that is exactly what this lurid rhus calls to mind. A very good gardener once told me to cut it almost to the ground in February, when the young growth would spring up in shoots as red as a garnet. One might treat oneself to two plants, reserving one of them for this rather brutal experiment.

August 21, 1955

The tall white lilies have been a tremendous stand-by in the June and July garden. Their cool splendour at twilight came like a draught of water after the hot day. I like to see them piercing up between low grey foliaged plants such as artemisia, southernwood, and santolina, and rising above some clouds of gypsophila, for there is something satisfying in the contrasting shapes of the domed bushes and the belfry-like tower of the lily; an architectural harmony.

Many people think lilies difficult to grow, and write them off as an expensive disappointment. This misconception must be due to several causes: (1) the notorious inverted snobbishness of the Madonna lily, which apparently refuses to flourish except in cottage gardens, (2) the prevalence of the fungus disease known as *botrytis* and the virus disease known as *mosaic*, (3) the belief that all lilies enjoy the same conditions, (4) the attempts of inexperienced gardeners to succeed with certain varieties which really defy all but the most expert handling. If the amateur, however, should content himself with half a dozen reliable kinds, triumph and not disappointment should be his.

*   *   *

In the first place he should acquaint himself with the likes and dislikes of the lilies he intends to grow. Some hate lime; others demand it. Secondly, he should make certain of buying nothing but sound bulbs, not dry or shrivelled bulbs, and never a bulb whose roots have been cut off. Cheap, rootless bulbs such as you often see in bins in shops and chainstores are almost certain to fail. Buy from a good nurseryman, and increase your stock by raising lilies from seed or scales, a most fascinating occupation. Thirdly, see to it that all lilies have good drainage; a pocket of sharp sand round each bulb will help a lot. Fourthly, I would say, start with the kinds that offer a reasonable hope of success, a short list in which the regal lily, *L. regale*, the Tiger lily, *L. tigrinum*, the yellow Turks cap, *L. pyrenaicum*, the purplish Turks cap, *L. martagon*, the vari-coloured *L. umbellatum* (or *hollandicum*) and the giant orange *L. henryi*, may safely figure.

I am aware that this list will bring a cry of derision from many successful experimenters. What about the Nankeen lily, *L. testaceum*, and what about the golden-rayed lily of Japan, *L. auratum*, and the panther lily, *L. pardalinum*, and even the immense Himalayan, *L. giganteum?* now to be called *Cardiocrinum giganteum*. Yes, I know, but if this article is not to stretch to an unprintable length I shall have to refer you to a practical little handbook which has just appeared, called *Lilies and their Cultivation*, by Mr. E. Leeburn, published by Messrs. Foyle, 119 Charing Cross Road, at 2s. 6d. For this modest price you cannot expect anything like the exhaustive *Lilies of the World*, by H. D. Woodcock and W. T. Stearn, or even *Lilies in their Homes*, by Mrs. A. C. Maxwell, at 35s. and 16s. respectively, but for simple instructions and easy reference it will prove indispensable to the amateur starting on his career or desirous of improving his present knowledge. I do wish, all the same, that the author could be induced to eliminate 98 per cent of his infuriating marks of exclamation.

August 25, 1957

Among the Bourbon roses, lack of space compelled me to omit *Mme Lauriol de Barny*, and indeed she is very large and proud. At a distance, but for the foliage, you might mistake her for a small peony. (I am aware that the French do not recognize her as a true Bourbon, but classify her under the curious name of hybrid *non-remontant*.) Dating back to 1868, she has all the rosy lavishness of ladies of the Second Empire. I wish I could find out who Mme Lauriol was in real life, to have so sumptuous a flower called after her. I suspect that she may have belonged to the *haute cocotterie* of Paris at that date, or possibly I misjudge her and she may have been the perfectly respectable wife of some M. de Barny, perhaps a rose-grower at Lyon. Someone ought to write the biographies of persons who have had roses named in their honour. Who was Mme Hardy? Who was Charles de Mills? I don't know, and I long for a Who's Who to correct my ignorance.

Souvenir de la Malmaison, 1843, is easier to place as to name, although Josephine Beauharnais can never have seen it. I suppose there will be screams if I say that this famous rose has never been one of my favourites. A perfect bloom, yes; but how often do we get one? It all too easily goes brown and sodden. The best thing I have to say for it is that it played its part in producing *Gloire de Dijon*, that fragrant crumpled straw-coloured old stager, equally charming as a climber or as a bush. *Variegata di Bologna* is a fairly recent production, 1909, and is said to be a strong grower on rich soils. It looks miserable in my garden, greatly to my regret, for I know of no other rose with its colouring: violet stripes on a white background. Mr. Graham Thomas suggests that it might do well under a north-west wall, with a cool root-run. No doubt I have planted it in too sunny a place.

This does not by any means exhaust the list of the Bourbon roses. I have omitted *la Reine Victoria*, who appeared in 1872, although I have mentioned her child, *Mme Pierre Oger. Mme E. Calvat* I have never seen, but know by repute as one of the best, pink and scented, and suitable for growing up a pillar. *Roi des pourpres*, now renamed *Prince Charles*, is not to my mind amongst the best of the violet or lilac roses; for this colour I would rather go to *Cardinal Richelieu*, a gallica, or *William Lobb*, a moss. Finally, *Blairi No. 2* is a most exquisite climber, rather a deep pink; I believe that its somewhat unexpected name is due to the fact that the

Mr. Blair who raised it and others in 1845 could not be bothered to find appropriate names for them all.

The Bourbon roses should not be heavily pruned, and indeed their full beauty can be displayed only when they are allowed to grow into the great tall bushes natural to them. Dead and twiggy wood should be cut out. How easy to say, and how scratchy to do.

August 26, 1956

Mid-August means the beginning of autumn, so we had better bravely make up our minds to it. Not that I have anything to say against autumn, as such. On certain days we may well be tempted to think it the most richly beautiful of seasons. It is only as a portent that we deplore it.

In a small square garden enclosed by holly hedges, I have been making notes of some plants in flower just now. They are all in the same range of colour—yellow, red, and orange —which explains why people often call it the sunset garden. At its best, it glows and flames. The dark hedges enhance the effect. Ideally, the hedges ought to be draped in ropes and curtains of the scarlet *Tropœolum speciosum*, the Flame Flower so rampant in the North; but this must be a Scottish Nationalist by conviction, for it will have little to say to Sassenach persuasions.

The rest of the little garden makes up for the lack. There are red-hot pokers, tiger lilies, montbretias, and that thing which looks like a giant montbretia, *Antholyza*, inevitably known as Aunt Eliza though nobody's Aunt Eliza could ever have looked so garish. The yellows are represented by the shrubby St. John's Wort, *Hypericum var. hidcote*; I know the Rowallane hypericum is better, but it isn't as hardy, and there doesn't seem much to choose between them. More yellows come in that coarse, tall, feathery groundsel, *Senecio tanguticum*, and in some gaillardias and in some belated yarrows and potentillas, with golden pansies as a ground-work in front of some Orange Bedder snapdragons. Some *Lilium henryi*, one of the easiest of lilies, rise taller than a tall man amongst rose bushes of *Mrs. Van Rossem*; a patch of zinnias gives a dash of orange just where it is needed; the dahlia Bishop of Llandaff sets its dark-green leaves and dark-red flower in a shady corner; the brilliance of the new hybrid, *Venidio-arctotis*, blazes in a narrow bed just where the sun strikes to make it open.

Have I exaggerated? Of course I have. The little garden was not quite like that, but it came very close to the idea, and there seems no reason why one day it should not fulfil the conception of its owner. That is the whole essence and excitement of gardening: to conceive a picture in the mind, and gradually year by year to improve it towards its completion.

August 28, 1955

Four months without rain, or so they tell me. Lying under the pine trees on a hillside in Tuscany, and gazing over a view which embraces the distant Apennines and the even more distant marble mountains of Carrara, I reflect as I have often reflected before on the advantages of the climate in that triangular northern island I left only yesterday. All along the roads here in Italy, it is true, the oleanders and the hibiscus are making a display we could never hope to rival; the stone pines and the olives are not for us; but what of the parched grass that has to be renewed annually to produce even the caricature of a lawn? What of the starved and dusty geraniums in pots, assiduously watered every evening and looking not a whit the better for it? No amount of watering ever took the place of a warm shower. Four months without rain.

No wonder that the designers of gardens in the great Italian villas have concentrated upon greenness. Green is the coolest of colours; it almost makes a shadow in itself, a grotto, a sanctuary from the glaring day. We in England are so well accustomed to the green of our turf and our trees that we take it for granted and turn for our delight to the bright colour of flowers as a relief under our dovelike skies. But in the south nothing is more grateful than the formalized green or clipped box, cavernous ilexes, aisles of cypress, mossy statuary, stone-edged pools, and the drip of a fountain trickling away into a little noisy runnel.

It was, however, about acacias that I really intended to write. Their correct name is *Robinia pseudacacia*, but as acacia is the current usage I let it stand. They abound in France and Italy, but are equally at home with us. There are few summer-flowering trees prettier than they, when they hang out their pale, sweet-scented tassels, and few faster of growth for people in a hurry. I have planted them no taller than a walking-stick, and within a contemptible number of years they have taken on the semblance of an established inhabitant, with sizeable trunks and a rugged bark and a spreading head, graceful and fringy. If they have a fault, it is that their boughs are brittle, that they make a good deal of dead wood, and, I suspect, are not very long-lived, especially if the main trunk has forked, splitting the tree into halves. This danger can be forestalled by allowing only one stem to grow up, with no subsidiary lower branches.

If, after reading this cautionary tale, you still decide to plant an acacia, let me suggest that you might try not only the ordinary white-flowered one, but also the lovely pink one, *Robinia hispida*, the rose acacia. It is no more expensive to buy than the white, and is something less often seen, a surprise to people who expect white flowers and suddenly see pink. *Robinia kelseyi* is another rose-pink form much to be recommended.

September

September 1, 1956

SOME two years ago I observed a brilliant showy plant growing in the prettiest of Scottish nursery gardens, Inshriarch, near Aviemore. I long to go back there. The garden had been carved out of a clearing in a wood of silver birch and dark green juniper; many little burns ran down channels cut in the peaty soil; primulas and gentians grew like weeds, though true weeds there were none. It was not only the prettiest but also the tidiest of nursery gardens, crammed with covetable things which I feared I could not grow with any success down here in the south-east of England.

I did, however, bring away a pot-grown plant of *Lychnis haageana*, the showy brilliant plant I referred to; and it has served me well. I would recommend it to everybody who wants a flare of colour for the front of the border or for the rock garden in July. I saved its seed, but need scarcely have troubled to do so, as it came up of its own accord in unexpected places, a most agreeable device for a plant which, although nominally a perennial, is apt to die out after a year or so. My original plant hasn't, yet, but has left so profuse a progeny that its departure into another world would not now matter, except that one is always sorry to say goodbye.

This would be the time to obtain ripe seed for sowing. I must warn prospective growers that this campion, the English name for lychnis, is variable when you grow it from seed. The seeds I saved and sowed threw flowers in different colours. Some of them came in the bright orange red of the flame of an oil-lamp, *lychnos* being the Greek word for a lamp. Some of them came much paler, straw-coloured; some came pale pink; and some a dull white. I scrapped the white; threw them out; kept the straw-coloured and the pink and left the rest to seed themselves and take a chance on their coming up in the show they will make, as I hope, next year.

They are rather untidy; their leaves are ugly; their flowers shaggy and tattered like a flag torn in a gale. But so gay, even as a flag flying 12 in. above the ground.

Truly, they are worth this recommendation. They got an Award of Merit from the R.H.S. in 1953, which is something worth having, a more valuable sanction than I could give.

Campions all, they belong to the same family as the Ragged Robin of our banks and woodlands, and as the tall, scarlet, rather coarse *Lychnis chalcedonica* so familiar once in old herbaceous borders and still not to be despised.

September 1, 1957

The Bourbon roses gave birth to the race of hybrid perpetuals, who in their turn were developed into the hybrid teas. The hybrid perpetuals have now become somewhat obsolete and superseded by the hybrid teas, a pity in my opinion since there are still some H.P.'s available and some of them are very useful for prolonging the season besides having the quality as lasting well in water. This is especially true of *Ulrich Brunner*, stiff-stemmed, almost thornless, cherry-red in colour, very prolific indeed, a real cut-and-come again.

These strong growers lend themselves to various ways of treatment. They can be left to reach their free height of 7 to 8 ft., but then they wobble about over eye-level and you can't see them properly, with the sun in your eyes, also they get shaken by summer gales. A better but more laborious system is to tie them down to benders, by which I mean flexible wands of hazel with each end poked firmly into the ground and the rose-shoots tied down at intervals, making a sort of half-hoop. This entails a lot of time and trouble, but is satisfactory if you can do it; also it means that the rose breaks at each joint, so that you get a very generous *floraison*, a lovely word I should like to see imported from the French into our language. If you decide to grow hybrid perpetuals on this system of pegging them down, you ought to feed them richly, with organic manure if you can get it, or with compost if you make it, but anyhow with something that will compensate for the tremendous effort they will put out from being encouraged to break all along their shoots. You can't ask everything of a plant, any more than you can exact everything of a human being, without giving some reward in return. Even the performing seal gets an extra herring.

Ulrich Brunner, Frau Karl Druschki, and the Dicksons, Hugh and George, are very suitable for this kind of training.

The hybrid perpetuals can also be used as wall plants; not nearly so tall as true climbers and ramblers, they are quite tall enough for, say, a space under a ground floor window; or they may be grown on post-and-wire as espaliers outlining a path. I once had a blood-red Dickson trained in the shape of a peacock's tail.

I find *Paul Neyron* described in one rosarian's catalogue as having 'the largest flowers we know among roses . . . suffused with an exquisite shade of lilac, with silver reverse,' and in another catalogue as having 'enormous rich pink flowers, fully double.' This sounds all right to me; I have long since learnt not to be misled by catalogue descriptions, but these are from two catalogues that I can trust. Moreover, *Paul Neyron* appears to be identical with, or indistinguishable from, the famous Rose de la Reine, raised in

1840 by M. Laffay, of Auteuil, who grew 200,000 seedling roses a year and took his chance of finding something really good amongst them.

That gives one to think.

September 4, 1955

I have never yet made up my mind about plants of variegated foliage. There was a time when I was arrogantly certain that I did not like them; could not abide them; was reminded of Victorian shrubberies; even of aspidistras in seaside lodging-houses. Such are the powers of association.

Now, I am not sure. One's taste alters; but whether it ameliorates or deteriorates is difficult to determine. There can be no Absolute in canons of taste; there are only standards, and although these should always be high they should never remain rigid. Mine, so far as concerns variegated foliage, are still in a state of flux. They waver, as reeds in a stream, but at least the stream is frisky and not stagnant.

These reflections have been unwittingly suggested to me by a correspondent who asks what things with 'light-coloured leaves' he could plant in his garden. I see what he means. He wants a silvery-looking small tree; let him plant the silver maple, *Acer saccharninum*.

There are many other maples, scarlet of leaf, only too familiar in small rock-gardens; I can see the irresistibility of their blood-red splash, especially when poised like a chamois on an eminence catching the rays of sunset, but am left with the uneasy conviction that they must really look their best in masses on their native hillsides in Japan and North America. If my correspondent, however, is bent upon getting away from the usual forms of *Acer palmatum* or *Acer negundo*, and wants a pale, grizzled, marbled, parti-coloured, mackerel version, let him turn his attention to *Acer negundo variegatum*, which will give green leaves with a white edging, or *A. negundo aureo-variegatum* which as its name implies gives leaves splotched with yellow. Any of these can be planted in little groups or as single specimens; some peat in the soil pleases them, and it is well to keep them away from frost if possible, not because of any tenderness in their constitution but because the young leaves are liable to damage from frost or cold winds, making them look seared and shabby. *

If it is not necessarily variegation that my correspondent requires, but merely a pale tree, he might try *Pyrus salicifolia pendula*. This is otherwise known as the willow-leafed pear, very grey, with white flowers in April, and a drooping habit not unlike a weeping willow. It should be grown as a single specimen, preferably in a place where you can walk all round it and admire its circularity. Extremely graceful, the tips of its long shoots can be clipped to prevent them from trailing on the ground.

September 8, 1957

A note on climbers may well conclude this series of suggestions about roses. Not always do we see the best use made of the many lovely varieties available, yet how wide is the scope, whether we plant against a wall, or over a bank, or up a pillar, or even an archway, or in that most graceful fashion of sending the long strands up into an old tree, there to soar and dangle, loose and untrammelled.

The rambling wichurianas are especially suited for such a purpose, since with one or two exceptions such as *Albertine* and *Albéric Barbier* they are apt to develop mildew on a wall, and prefer the air to blow freely through them. *Félicité et Perpétue*, commemorating two young women who suffered martyrdom at Carthage in A.D. 203, will grow at least 20 ft. high into the branches, very appropriately, since St. Perpetua was vouchsafed the vision of a wonderful ladder

---

* Mr. C. J. Marchant, whose address will be found on p. 195 of this book, has a fine list of maples.

reaching up to heaven. *François Juranville* and *Léontine Gervais*, both pink-and-buff, hang prettily, if less vigorous of growth. Among other wichurianas, of a stiffer character than the ramblers, *The New Dawn* and *Dr. Van Fleet* are to my mind two of the best, very free-flowering throughout the summer, of a delicate but definite rose-pink. *Emily Gray*, reputed tender though I have never found her so, planted on a south-facing wall, large single pale yellow flowers, and dark green shiny leaves; *Cupid*, a hybrid tea, pink with a gold central boss; and *Elegance*, white and gold, are all very much to be recommended. *Mermaid* is perhaps too well known to be mentioned, but should never be forgotten, partly for the sake of the pale-yellow flowers, opening flat and single, and partly because of the late flowering season, which begins after most other climbers are past their best. I must add that *Mermaid* should be regarded with caution by dwellers in cold districts.

Where the choice is so wide it becomes difficult to include all that certainly deserve inclusion, but I must mention *Allen Chandler*, a magnificent red, only semi-double, which carries some bloom all through the summer. Not, I think, a rose for a house of new brick, but superb on grey stone, or on white-wash, or indeed any colour-wash. If you want a white rose, flushed pink, scented, very vigorous and seldom without flowers, try *Mme Alfred Carrière*,* best on a sunny wall but tolerant of a west or even a north aspect; and if a yellow rose, very deep yellow, plant *Lawrence Johnston*, of which it must, however, be said that the first explosion of bloom is not usually succeeded by many subsequent flowers.

Finally, remember that most of the favourite hybrid teas may be obtained in climbing forms, including the in-my-opinion horridly coarse but ever-popular *Peace*.

September 9, 1956

Everybody who moves about the countryside by road must have noticed what pretty effects have recently been obtained by the use of colour-wash and paint. I suppose it is a reaction against the drabness of the war years. We had to remain dingy, or else go gay. We have chosen to go gay, and some of our cottages and minor houses now look as cheerfully bright and southern as anything in Spain or Provence.

Gardeners can do much to supplement this transformation. I have one or two particular instances in mind. One of them is a lime-washed cottage in a village street, simple as can be, where the occupier has trained a few strands of a rose-red Japanese quince against the white wall; for purity of outline and sharpness of colour it could rival the most sparse and precious of Japanese flower-arrangements. Later on in the year, the fruits hang jade-green along the branches.

Then there is a garage on a hillside. The one-car garage attached to a new bungalow is not usually an object giving pleasure to the eye, but this one has been magicked into a toy as pretty as any dolls' house. Painted white, with turquoise-blue doors and surrounds to the windows, pale pink geraniums pour from window-boxes and some greenery creeps in chosen design across the white. It cannot have been an expensive treatment. It demanded only some imagination to transform a utilitarian functional object such as a ready-made garage into an eyeful of surprised pleasure.

If some people of taste and imagination can accomplish these things, why can't we all, and do our tiny part in saving our country from the vandalism that threatens it?

This is perhaps not a very practical article. I have not suggested a single thing to grow in your garden. So here is an idea. I thought that if you had a front-door without a porch, it might be amusing to grow an apple or a pear which in time would form a deep porch framing the door. You would have to plant one on either side, trained on wires to meet overhead. I have never seen this done, but I don't see why not. And if you felt even more enterprising, and had a south aspect, you might substitute peaches. A young tree of the peach called Peregrine has astonished me this year with its huge juicy fruits. What fun, to have peaches ripe for the picking, on a summer morning for breakfast.

September 11, 1958

One of the most beautiful of early-autumn flowering bulbs is surely the Scarborough lily. That is its everyday name, but botanically it is known as *Vallota purpurea* or *Vallota speciosa*. Like the Belladonna lily, it belongs to the family of the Amaryllidaceae, and comes from South Africa, not from Scarborough. (See also p. 50, March 24, 1957.) Usually regarded as a pot plant for the cool greenhouse, there has long been some dispute as to its hardiness; William Robinson way back in the 1880's remarked that the outdoor culture of this plant deserved more attention than it had hitherto received, and Mr. E. A. Bowles in 1915 recorded that he had grown it successfully for three seasons in the open, until a wet autumn and cold winter killed the whole lot so remorselessly that he never ventured on another trial. All this points to the conclusion that if you want to grow it out of doors you should give it the warmest possible place, say at the foot of a south wall, and plant it fairly deep, say 6 in., with a generous allowance of sand, and a covering of bracken or pine branches in winter. Like the Belladonna lily, it appreciates water when the leaves begin to appear but should be kept on the dry side during its resting period, from November to March or April, advice which is more easily followed when the bulbs are grown in pots under glass. Grown out of doors, a cloche or handlight might be the solution.

Kept in pots it gives little trouble, as it does not need constant repotting, but seems rather to enjoy becoming cramped in a pot that you might imagine too small for so large a bulb.

The colour is variously described as scarlet or bright scarlet, a description I find most misleading, almost as misleading as the botanical adjective *purpurea*. Scarlet may be the official term on the R.H.S. colour chart, but to my mind it suggests a Guardsman's tunic or the zonal pelargonium so aptly named Grenadier. The Scarborough lily has far more orange in it. Allowing for the difference in texture between a hard substance and the soft translucent petal of a flower, it exactly resembles coral. I have held them side by side to compare, and if only a stray bloom of the *chaenomeles* Knaphill Scarlet would make its appearance at this time of year, as sometimes happens, I fancy that I should find very little difference in colour. But there again, this variety of *chaenomeles* is dubbed scarlet, so evidently I am at variance with the authorities, and, unrepentant, shall remain so.

September 15, 1957

The vast family of primulas contains some of the loveliest and most reliable of plants, ranging from the pale primrose of our woods to the tall Asiatics and their hybrids, about which I propose to write today. Generally speaking, this class or group enjoys a moist soil and a shady place; and as there is a constant demand for plants that will thrive in shade, awkward to satisfy, the primulas will be found very useful as well as beautiful.

Of them all, I least like *Florindae*, the Tibetan cowslip, with its somewhat untidy drooping yellow bells, but it is a fool-proof plant of amazing vigour, setting so much seed that you could naturalize it anywhere by scattering it in handfuls or by transplanting clumps of the innumerable seedlings. There are hybrid forms, mostly in rosy-brick red which I greatly prefer to the original type. *Primula japonica* and *Primula pulverulenta* are perhaps the most familiar to the amateur gardener; the Bartley strain of *pulverulenta*, downy, and softly coloured like a ripe peach, is one of my favourites, but I find it hard to choose between the Asthore hybrids, and *bulleyana* orange-yellow, and *sikkimensis* pale-yellow, and *chionantha*, ivory-white as cream.

There are many others of the shade-loving moisture-loving primulas. Once you start on them, there seems to be no end. Don't we all know the mauve *denticulata*, and *capitata mooreana*, and the little low-growing *rosea* which will increase itself all over the place where it finds itself happy? What a wonderful and varied plant family this is, some of them coming from such remote regions as the high mountains of Central Asia, and one our own tiny native *farinosa*, the bird's-eye primrose, snuggling along the banks of the becks of our northern moors.

I cannot mention them all; nor even half that I would like to mention. I can suggest only that you should get a catalogue from a nurseryman specializing in primulas, such as Mr. H. P. Lyall, Mount Pleasant Lane, Bricket Wood, Watford, and make a choice depending upon his descriptions and according to the soil and aspect you are able to provide. There is something suitable for nearly all situations, including the rock garden. Remember also that many can be grown from seed, and that fully grown plants can be increased by division immediately after they have flowered, usually about July. These easy methods of propagation make for considerable economy in raising a stock and when you consider the variety of colour and the general accommodating habit of this lovely race, I feel sure you will at least give them a trial in your garden.

September 16, 1956

The great family of the Narcissi is surely one of the most dependable. Wheresoever you plant them, the bulbs never fail to throw up the flower already conceived inside them, going on year after year, increasing in quantity until they begin to deteriorate in quality, when you can dig them up and make two score where you once planted one. There is something very satisfactory in lifting a huge clump by spade from the turf, and dividing the children of those brown onions from their parents, to grow on into a new plump life of their own.

I called them narcissi, for there is really no difference between the daffodil and the narcissus. It is simply a distinction popularly made between Trumpet and Flat-face. This is putting it very crudely, but for practical purposes it will serve. Whichever sort you intend to plant, the sooner you do it the better. October is not too late, but September is better still. If you want exhibition blooms, you will plant them in bare beds; but if you want a drift looking right and happy, you will fling a handful over a stretch of grass and plant them where they fall and roll. Never mind if their distribution seems irregular as the bulbs lie waiting on top of the ground. It will look all right when they come up next March.

For my own part, I like to see them growing in groups of separate varieties, rather than mixed. There are now so many varieties that the choice becomes bewildering, also slight differences in price for which I must refer you to the catalogues. Very roughly speaking, prices range from 7s. to 14s. a dozen. Here are a few trumpet daffodils that I would not be without: Golden Harvest, Magnificence, Rembrandt, all yellow, and in the cheaper yellows I remain faithful to King Alfred and Winter Gold, although I know the experts regard them as having been superseded. If you like the purity of white trumpets, you could not do better than

Mount Hood; the more familiar white Beersheba, lovely though she is, tends to flop on her stalk and is preferable as a cut flower than naturalized in the garden. The old so-called pink daffodil, Mrs. R. O. Backhouse, is a slight favourite of mine, and has dropped in price to 12s. a dozen.

Among the large-cupped narcissi, Fortune is still one of the best, at 8s. a dozen; I believe when it first appeared on the market it cost £500 a bulb. John Evelyn, ivory white, I have found to be a tremendous increaser, so very good for naturalizing though not much good for picking. Carlton is a fine and faithful golden-yellow. Aranjuez, with a yellow perianth widely edged in deep orange-red, is cheap at 10s. 6d., and suffers from nothing but its name, at which the English are apt to make a bad shy shot sounding like Arran-juice. I must end this very short list with La Riante, well named, for it really does seem to laugh with all the gaiety of spring.

I have not even mentioned the tinies of the family, a nursery-party, such as *cyclamineus*, *bulbocodium*, jonquils, and narcissus *triandrus* or Angel's Tears. I hope to return to these next week, for it is not yet too late to plant them. *

September 18, 1955

A full-stop or exclamation mark is often of extreme importance in a garden, something which will arrest the eye and give emphasis to some focal point. For this purpose nothing could be more effective than the Irish yew, which with its erect fastigiate habit may well be considered as taking the place of the cypress in this country. It can be kept as neat and slender as any cypress, for many years, by a judicious tying-in of its branches from early youth until it reaches its eventual height of some 20 ft. or more. Even when quite young, only 5 or 6 ft. high, the little pointed

* See p. 151, September 23, 1956.

tree looks agreeably mature, an impression doubtless due to the sobriety of its dark attire and the serious uprightness of its demeanour.

Is the story of its origin too well known to bear repetition? It seems to have appeared as a chance seedling of our common native yew, *Taxus baccata*, and was found nearly 200 years ago by a Mr. Willis on his farm in the hills of Co. Fermanagh. Mr. Willis was shrewd enough to notice the difference. He retained one of his two seedlings and gave the other to his landlord at Florence Court where it still survives, the matriarchal ancestress of any Irish yew now awaiting your order in a nursery garden.

* * *

The well-informed reader may here object that some young trees were found growing wild in Sussex in the first decade of this century, when nobody knew how they had come there, but these were male trees and who can say they were not a garden escape?

It may be useful to remark, for the benefit of those who grow yews or a yew hedge in their garden and who have observed a distressing sooty blackness spreading over their trees, that this dirty infection is readily curable by spraying in September and March with an emulsion of white oil and nicotine. It is due to a scale insect, which may be discovered as a tiny brown patch on the underside of the leaves and whose excrement produces the mould rightly named Sooty Mould, for you might as well handle the gear of a chimney-sweep. The excrement itself is known as honey-dew; sad that so lovely a word should be afflicted with so unsavoury a meaning.

The scale should be got rid of as quickly as possible, and if the yews have already suffered to any serious extent they should be fed back into health. Dried blood or a special yew fertiliser called Taxus are both excellent, or you can dust round each plant with a handful of nitrate of soda, mixed with sand, in April, May, or June. This should perhaps be regarded as a stimulant rather than a food. Do not allow the mixture to touch either the stem or the leaves.

September 22, 1957

All writers of gardening articles must be uneasily aware of their own patches of ignorance. Lucky for them if their patches do not run into acres. My own worst worry runs into several million acres, for it covers the whole of London and every other city in the British Isles. In other words, I am at a loss to know how to answer the wistful letters asking what to do with a town garden.

I always thought the answer must be rather depressing. The town gardener has to contend with dirty soil, absence of sunlight, smog, and his neighbours' cats. Not unwarrantably is the usual town garden described as a cat-run. However, a book I have just been reading holds out more hope for the town gardener than I ever believed possible, and the many photographs illustrating existent town gardens should convince everybody that success does not dwell only in the author's mind.

It appears, supported by these photographs, that a surprising lot of plants can be made to flourish, given a reasonable amount of care. There are certain things every town gardener knows: that irises will do; that jasmine will climb rather sootily; that flowering trees such as almonds, acacias, laburnums, prunuses, will enliven many a front or even a back yard; that the bulbs of crocus, snowdrop, daffodil, hyacinth, tulip, are more or less dependable; but how many perplexed householders realize that they can also grow such delectably countrified objects as culinary herbs, herbaceous plants, hollyhocks, Morning Glory, Heavenly Blue, green hellebores, roses as climbers or ramblers, standards or bushes, wistaria and clematis scrambling over dividing walls, some honeysuckles, foliage plants for a shady corner, forsythia to go golden in the spring, vines to go red in the autumn—there seems no end to the possibilities.

This is not a cheap book. It costs two guineas. It would make a perfect present for a town-gardening friend. It has been written out of long experience by a man who, in collaboration with his wife, to whom he accords the warmest generous acknowledgement, has worked to create what is probably the most imaginative garden in the heart of London. He knows all the difficulties, he knows all the problems. He sympathizes with other people who have little more than a cat-run or back yard to turn into something suggesting the country cottage garden they once knew or dreamt of.

The book I have been reading, and which has cheered me up so much as to the answers I can in future return, is called *Successful Town Gardening*, by Lanning Roper, published by Country Life Ltd., 42s.

September 23, 1956

At the end of my article last Sunday (September 16, 1956), p. 148, I referred to the tinies of the narcissus family and said I would return to them. I suppose I ought to start with the tiniest of all, *minimus*, a little yellow trumpet no more than 3 in. high, which likes peat but hates manure, and is perhaps seen at its best in a pan on the staging of a cold greenhouse, where it will not get splashed or dashed by February weather and can be appreciated at a convenient eye level. In fact, all the miniature narcissi make pretty pot plants if a few bulbs can be spared for that purpose, though all of them are hardy and can be grown out-of-doors, on a rockery, or in a trough, or naturalized in grass.

The very strongly scented ones gain by the more intimate position of a pan on the staging. The Pyreneean *juncifolius* certainly does, for the fragrance of its 6-in.-high bright yellow flowers, rising amongst rush-like leaves, would be wasted on the open air. *Juncifolius* is a treasure, cheap at 5s. 6d. a dozen, and well worth one panful as a treat.

The *bulbocodium* or hoop-petticoat daffodil is an easy one, which you may have seen naturalized in grass almost by the acre at Wisley, and very pretty it is, small and tight-waisted, springing out into a crinoline. It does not like to be too dry, and the same may be said of *cyclamineus*, which lays its ears back as though frightened or in a tantrum, like the small cyclamens. *Narcissus triandrus albus*, called Angel's Tears, also lays its ears back. Ivory-white, about 6 in. high, most delicately pretty, it will grow in broken shade, where it looks like a little ghost, weeping.

This is a very short list, and I haven't yet mentioned the jonquils. Do not be misled by the variety listed as *odorus* or *odoratus*. They are far less odorous than the plain simple single jonquil, throwing up its yellow flower between rush-like leaves. Get the single jonquil every time, it is far more sweetly scented than the double varieties, and makes a graceful fragrant bowl planted in fibre to put on a table indoors, or can be planted out of doors when you can pick a bunch for a vase. These scented things give their best when you can see them closely and smell them closely. Out in the open, the scent is lost, though their blowing bending delicacy is a lovely sight when ruffled by a breeze. Which reminds me to mention that innocent, our own Lent lily, still to be seen, I believe, in certain meadows and on certain hill-sides where it has so far escaped the plough. We should plant it in order to ensure its survival.

September 25, 1957

It occurred to me, after writing last week (September 18, 1955, pp. 148–9) about the Irish yew, that some people nourish a prejudice against yews. They think them funereal. This is purely a question of association, because yews are often found in churchyards, but people have their prejudices, and it is no good arguing against them. 'A man convinced against his will, is of the same opinion still,' so if people don't like the dark yew in their garden let me suggest a substitute, the Irish juniper, *J. hibernica* or *fastigiata*, which possesses the same rigid columnar shape, equally valuable as the fullstop or exclamation mark I recommended for a focal point, but less severe and grim, being blue-green, almost glaucous, in colour, not that dark almost black-green that some people find so gloomy. Personally, I like all gloomy trees; perhaps I have a melancholy streak in my character; anyhow, I like the dark background they make, reminding me of cypresses in Italy and of stone-pines in Spain.

The junipers have many advantages. For one thing, they are lime-lovers, meaning that owners of gardens on an alkaline chalky soil can plant them with every hope of success. This does not imply that they will not grow elsewhere: I have seen a creeping juniper, a spreading type, growing in peaty soil in Scotland, ramping wild all over a woodland stretch under silver birches. I brought home an armful of its dead branches, and used them as smouldering pokers to push into a wood-fire on my hearth, waving them about the room as one would wave old stalks of lavender or rosemary, redolent as incense but far fresher and less heavy on the air. I took this to be *J. horizontalis*, apparently the only variety which does not favour a limestone soil, but on enquiry discovered that it was the common juniper, dwarfed by deer and rabbits eating it in the winter.

It made a beautiful, stiff, dark carpet under the pallor of the silver birches. Little burns dribbled, in a natural irrigation. Their bubbles rose like bursting pearls over the shallow pebbles. It made me wish to possess not a more-or-less-formal but a completely informal garden, with wild woodland on the margin. I don't mean to complain about my own garden. It serves me and satisfies me quite well, except at the moments when I get into despair over it; very frequent moments, when I long to have some other sort of garden, quite different; a garden in Spain, a garden in Italy, a garden in Provence, a garden in Scotland.

One can't have everything, and one mustn't be too greedy. Committed as I am to a more-or-less-formal garden, I would very strongly recommend the Irish juniper to anyone who wants a full-stop focal point where it seems necessary. It has an architectural value, of great importance in even the smallest acreage.

September 29, 1957

There is no doubt that the gladioli are very useful in providing colour at a time of year when flowers are becoming scarce. They are as showy as the dahlia and far less of a nuisance, for I have proved to my satisfaction over a number of years that they can be left in the ground through the winter—yes, even the winter of 1956—and will reappear at the appropriate moment. There was a colony I did not much like, and could not be bothered to dig up and store, so left them to take their chance, almost hoping that they would miss it; but there they were again, and have been ever since. I suppose the corms had originally been planted fairly deep, at least 6 to 8 in., and thus escaped the hardest freezing of the ground.

I know that what I am saying goes against all orthodox advice, but can only record my own experience. Don't blame me if it goes wrong for you.

My chief grievance against the gladiolus is that its flower-spike comes out at the bottom before it comes out at the top. For all I know, some botanist in South Africa, New Zealand, Canada, California, or the British Isles may now be busy working on the production of a Sword-flower which will open all the way up at the same time, instead of staggering its yearly autumnal holiday over several weeks. Any hybridizer who could produce such an unstaggered gladiolus would surely make his fortune.

I like calling the gladiolus the Sword-flower. The name goes right back to the elder Pliny, who gave it that name as a diminutive of *gladius*, a sword; Pliny, a gardener and a naturalist, who got overwhelmed by the eruption of Vesuvius over Pompeii, 1,878 years ago.

Pliny would certainly have been amazed by our twentieth-century garden hybrids. He might, and probably would, have preferred them to the species indigenous to the Mediterranean, which is all he can have known. I should disagree with Pliny: I like the little gladioli far better than the huge things so heavy that they need staking. I like the *primulinus* and the so-called *butterfly* gladioli, in their soft colouring and their hooded habit of turning back a petal, rather after the fashion of a cyclamen. I remember—could I ever forget?—picking a bunch of little wild gladioli at sunset off a mountain in Persia and putting them in a jam-jar on the wooden crate that served as our supper-table in our camping place.

They made all the garden hybrids look more vulgar than Hollywood.

September 30, 1956

How disobliging plants are, in so far as they will not willingly agree to move when one wants them to. One sees, in a friend's garden, the very thing one has been hunting for in vain. Fellow-gardeners being, as a rule, the most generous of people, one is instantly promised 'a rooted bit when I divide in the autumn,' and how often does that rooted bit fail to arrive. It is no lack of good will, but sheer forgetfulness. One could, of course, write a reminder, but either one doesn't like to bother or else one has oneself forgotten. How much better if one could carry off the desired bit, then and there.

It is sometimes possible. Experienced gardeners have a theory that it doesn't matter so much *when* you move a plant as *how* you move it. Up to a point, I agree. I am no great believer in the green fingers mystique; I think every finger, all eight of them, ten if you include the thumbs, has to be attached by some string to the information-office in the brain. In other words, you can't rely on a cheerfully optimistic instinct unsupported by no knowledge at all. Thus the experienced gardener knows that he must instantly cover up the freshly exposed roots, even with a sheet from today's newspaper, to the annoyance of anyone who hasn't yet read the paper, anything rather than let fibrous roots dry out in the air. He wraps them at once, within one minute; he would use his handkerchief, or tear a bit off the tail of his shirt, if nothing else were available. I have even seen a handful of damp grass or leaves wrapped round and secured with twine. Then he will rush his treasure home, and plant it, possibly puddling it in if he thinks it needs a drink, and in all cases will shade it from the sun for the first few days until it has re-established itself after its upheaval. An inverted flowerpot provides a simple protection for any small plant or rooted fragment.

Far be it from me to scoff wholly at the green fingers legend. Much truth has gone to the making of many legends. But I do contend that most of these old wives' tales of Granny who could make everything grow, no matter how she stuck it in, or however rough she treated it, were based on common sense and an observation of nature. Granny had absorbed certain elementary principles, not from books but from noticing what happened to plants and what they required. Her science did not take us all the way, not all the long way modern investigation is leading us, but at any rate she led us for some distance along the right sort of garden path.

October

I SHOULD like, with or without permission, to write two successive articles about the type of rose now called *floribunda*. It is too large a subject to cram into one article, for there can be no doubt that the floribundas are going to prove an immense value. We used to know them, or their originators, as the polyantha roses, when our acquaintance with the type was mostly limited to the Poulsen family: all those daughters called *Karen*, *Kirsten*, and *Elsa*, and even *Elsa's Rival*, described as an improvement on *Elsa*, which must have led to a lot of trouble in the feminine Poulsen nursery. Sisters do not always agree, and to have a sister called your rival must have come very hard on Elsa.

The Poulsens quickly achieved a wide popularity. No new villa garden was without them. They had their virtues, their undeniable virtues. They flowered continuously, and they made a show. What a show they made! Bright pink, bright scarlet, they were as inescapable as they were ubiquitous. One saw them everywhere, until one got sick of the sight of them. We have now progressed beyond them and have a far wider choice to range over.

The floribundas have all the virtues of the old polyanthas, with many virtues added. If you have not tried them yet, I urge you to do so without delay. As I said, I am dividing one article into two, and am putting the self-coloured in the first lot. For a rich dark red, plant *Frensham* and *Dusky Maiden* and *Donald Prior* and *Alain*. For a good yellow,

plant *Goldilocks*, and if you want a huge pink, plant *August
Seebauer*, a surprise to me when first it exploded in June
and went on producing its great flowers mixing themselves
in amongst the grey-green leaves of the shrubby Californian
poppy *Romneya coulteri*, a perfect combination of pink and
grey. *August Seebauer* is not so well known as it deserves
to be, so let me recommend it specially.

Then, since I am still on the subject of the self-coloured
floribundas, there is little *Fashion*, pretty as can be in the
pointed shrimp-pink bud and just as pretty when the bud
opens into the never-vulgar, slightly scented expansion of
the flower. *Fashion* is a darling, a floribunda for anybody
with appreciation of shape, colour, and subtlety in a rose.

October 6, 1957

'Sometimes I sits and thinks, and sometimes I just sits.'
The practising gardener seldom finds time to do either. He,
or she, is too busy weeding or staking or tying up things
that have fallen over or been blown down, or cutting hedges,
or planting bulbs for next spring. The major disadvantage
of having a garden, and working in it, is that one leaves
oneself with no leisure to study the result one has laboriously
achieved, or more likely failed to achieve. The practising
gardener is always a Martha; it is Mary who sits back in
admiration, saying how pretty that looks! Mary thinks it has
just happened, as a gift from Heaven; Mary is a dreamer;
Martha is a realist, knowing the practical pains and trouble
that have gone to the making of the effect Mary admires.
Mary can just sit. Martha, if she can spare the time for it,
can and must sit and think.

This sitting-and-thinking is very valuable at this time of
year. It is valuable at any time of year, in a garden, when
you want to make notes on the mistakes and omissions you
observe, but it is especially valuable in autumn, which is
the time for shifting plants to other positions or ordering

new plants from a nursery to fill up some gap you may now record. I spend quite a lot of time gazing round my garden and making notes of my mistakes and of my good intentions for the future. I sits and thinks, and I puts down the results of my thinks in a large note-book, under different headings which with any luck I shall remember to consult later on, a practice I would recommend to any fellow-gardener.

There are plants to be scrapped. I feel sure that one of the secrets of good gardening is always to remove, ruthlessly, any plant one doesn't like. Heart-breaking though it may be to chop down a tree one planted years ago, it is the right thing to do if that tree is now getting in the way and keeping the sun off something else that needs it. And so with everything: scrap what does not satisfy and replace it by something that will.

I feel sure also that the autumn is the time to look closely at the shapes and forms of shrubs and trees in their setting. Even in the smallest garden there is probably some branch that would be better lopped off, some shrub that would look better with some discipline and control. Shape, in a garden, is so important, if we regard, as I think we should, gardening as an extension of architecture; in other words, the garden as an outdoor extension of the house.

Gardening is endlessly experimental, and that is the fun of it. You go on trying and trying, testing and testing, and sometimes you have failures but sometimes you have successes which more than make up for the failures.

October 7, 1956

We do not make nearly enough use of the upper storeys. The ground floor is just the ground, the good flat earth we cram with all the plants we want to grow. We also grow some climbers, which reach to the first-floor windows, and we may grow some other climbers over a pergola, but our inventiveness usually stops short at that. What we tend to forget is that nature provides some far higher reaches into which we can shoot long festoons whose beauty gains from the transparency of dangling in mid-air.

What I mean, briefly, is things in trees:—

> The gadding vine, and ivy never sere.*

For example, ivy. I am no great lover of the adhesive ivy glueing itself to walls in a dark, dowdy, dusty mass and mess full of old birds'-nests which ought to be cleared out. As Milton rightly remarked, ivy is never sere. Sometimes one wishes it were. One gets so bored by its persistent stuffy evergreen. I would suggest growing one of the variegated ivies up into a tree instead, where its white-and-green or gold-and-green can hang loosely from the branches, becoming almost diaphanous with the light around it. I know I shall be told that ivy strangles trees, and I may also be told that only a giraffe would notice anything unusual; still, I proffer the advice.

There is no need to stick to ivy. The gadding vine will do as well. The enormous shield-shaped leaves of *Vitis coignettiae*, turning a deep pink in autumn, amaze us with their rich cornelian in the upper air, exquisitely veined and rosy as the pricked ears of an Alsatian dog. Then, if you prefer June-July colour to October colour, there is that curious vigorous climber, *Actinidia kolomitka*, which starts off with a wholly green leaf, then develops white streaks and a pink tip, and puzzles people who mistake its colouring habits for some new form of disease. Cats like it: and so do I, although I don't like cats.

October 9, 1955

To continue with my remarks on the floribunda roses. Last Sunday (October 2, 1955, p. 157), I confined myself to the self-coloured: the dark red, the pink, the yellow, and the curious shrimp-pink of my little favourite, *Fashion*. This

---

* Yes, I know this is a misquotation.

Sunday I would like to indicate some of the queer mixtures
this race supplies.

Masquerade, for instance. *Masquerade* seems to be becoming fairly well known, and I don't wonder. It is a real
catch-the-eye, throwing clusters of pink, red, yellow, and
orange, all on the same stalk and at the same time, as
though it had not decided which colour to favour and had
decided to try them all. The effect is as gay as any flag; in
fact one feels that it ought to be blazoned in the proud
heraldic terms: *or* and *gules*, not merely yellow and red. A
very strong grower, apparently immune from many of the
troubles that affect roses: black-spot, mildew, and all the
rest of the horrible tribe of spores and aphides that we have
to contend with. *Masquerade* has a companion in *United
Nations*. I don't like *United Nations* so well, but it is good
enough to be recommended. Some wag or wit must have
thought up that name for so multi-coloured a rose.

Many centuries ago the Persians budded three differently
coloured roses on one bush, but I must not waste my short
space here on so romantic a story.

Let me come back to some of the floribundas we can now
order and grow successfully in our gardens. There are the
Pinocchios. I cannot help thinking of the pinocchios as a
family of father and sons, even as I think of the Poulsens
as a family of sisters. Do not ask my why. There is *Pinocchio*
himself, pink, tight in his cluster. He has a central flower,
with lots of smaller flowers hugging round him, like a hen
surrounded by her chickens, only in this case he is their
father, not their mother. He is rightly named *Pinocchio*,
because in Italian *pinocchio* means a fir-cone, and that suggests something lovingly packed, nestling close, as Papa (or
should I say Babbo?) Pinocchio does for his family. He has
produced a son called *Lavender pinocchio*, a brownish-
mauve, like a bruise on the flesh coming out after the third
day. Some people call it morbid; but I like it very much

indeed, having peculiar tastes. *Yellow pinocchio* is a more cheerful little son, a gay little boy that nobody could object to. And there is also a white virginal daughter; I have not seen her yet, but she sounds as desirable as either of her brothers. She calls herself *White pinocchio.* *

October 14, 1956

The amateur gardener finds an endless fascination in watching the procedure of the professional. The employer of labour, if he be garden-minded, will stop to pull up a seeding groundsel. Not so his employee. Any timid suggestion that a certain corner is getting into rather a mess and hadn't something better be done about it, is instantly countered by the reply 'I haven't got round this way yet.' Murmurs about one year's seeds meaning seven years' weeds are of no avail. He hasn't got round that way yet, and nothing will get him round before he means to.

The same observation applies to the annual clipping of hedges. By the end of the summer, when clipping time arrives, hedges of yew and box have become so fluffy as to add to the slatternly appearance of the September garden. One longs to see them resume their sharp outlines, and the snip-snap of the shears one morning is the most welcome sound one could hear. But where has the man started on his job? Not at the front of the hedge, where it shows, oh no. One discovers him hidden somewhere at the invisible back, where it least matters, and one knows that it will be days or even weeks before he reappears to human view. One tries to explain this curious habit by thinking that he wants to get the dullest part over first, saving up the more amusing and repaying part for, so to speak, a treat. One could not be more mistaken. The professional's attitude towards his work is not fun, but plod. Impatience is unknown to him as it is not, alas, known only too well to you and me.

* I have got her now, and find her charming.

There must be a reason. I shall be told that t̶
is Method. You waste more time 'dodging about'
going to work methodically. This contention has
been evolved by the experience of generations, an̶
too much respect to dispute it. At the same time, n̶ ̶ ̶w̶e̶
not plead for a little more elasticity? There is, for example,
the question of seed-growing. Those pansy seeds, which
arrived a month ago, have not yet gone in: why not? 'I
haven't got round to seed-sowing yet.' In vain do we point
out that the matter is one of urgency; if the pansies are de-
layed much longer, the season will be past. 'All in good time,'
he says; 'all in good time. I've got the celery to earth up.'

It would seem, on the whole, as though we had something
to learn from him and he had something to learn from us.
A little less yielding to temptation on our part (that bit of
groundsel) and a little less rigidity on his (those seven years'
weeds). There can be few happier collaborations, properly
managed, than between an employer and his gardener; a
pity if they should ever be allowed to degenerate into a
source of mutual exasperation.

October 16, 1955

By the time this article appears in print I shall, I hope,
be far away in that delectable region of south-west France,
the Dordogne, the Lot, the Tarn, the Ariège, but before
I go I would like to leave a tribute to a rapid, little-used
climber, the Hop. We have our vast hop-gardens, here in
Kent where I live, and from the last week in August to
the third week in September our countryside suffers and
enjoys the Cockney invasion of hop-pickers, picturesque as
any vintage of grapes in southern countries. Alas, modern-
ization is catching up with even this traditional festivity,
and huge engines the size of threshing-machines on many
progressive farms now cruelly tear the delicate flowers from
the bines with talons of sharp steel.

This, however, is not what I intended to write about. I meant to suggest to anybody who has got a rough hedge, say of thorn or privet, or any old hedge that he cannot afford to grub, but would like to clothe with something pleasing and unusual, to grow through it and across it during the summer, why not grow the hop? Some hop-plants appeared accidentally in just such a hedge bordering my garden, and I accepted them with delight. I should never have thought of planting them deliberately; they came of their own accord; and how grateful I have been to them ever since.

Let me enumerate their virtues.

(1) They grow as fast as any annual climber, such as Morning Glory or *Cobaea scandens*.

(2) Unlike those two, they are not annual but perennial, and will duly shoot up again year after year.

(3) They can be used as a quick climber over a pergola, to fill up gaps while you wait for your better climbers to mature; in fact, I can imagine a pergola clothed in nothing but hops, and very pretty it might be. The leaf is of a fine design, and when the flower comes later it has all the dangling though far less ponderous beauty of a bunch of muscat grapes.

(4) You can make hop-pillows, stuffed with the dried flowers, very helpful to sufferers from insomnia.

(5) Finally, though perhaps I ought to have put this first in seasonal succession, you can pick young hop-shoots in March or April and use them as a vegetable. There is no waste in so doing, because every hop-hill will throw up far more shoots than it can carry, and the superfluous shoots have to be pruned away. The waste occurs only because few English house-wives or cooks realize that here they have a free supply of something that has a taste closely resembling fresh asparagus. *

* A warning footnote. Hop-roots, properly called hop-hills, cannot be bought from any nurseryman. They have to be obtained from a local farmer or hop grower.

October 21, 1956

How envious one feels of the terraced hillsides of the south, for there are few more delightful or satisfactory forms of gardening than dry-wall gardening. Plants can run their roots right back into the cool soil between stones, finding every drop of moisture even in a dry season, and can open their faces to the sun on the wall-front. I write these words in Spain, wishing that I could bring home even one length of the rough walling, probably many hundreds of years old, a sad sight now where phylloxera has destroyed the vines and the frosts of last February nearly killed the grey olives. They are shooting again from the base, but it will be ten years and more before they return to full bearing.

*   *   *

English people who live in a stone country such as the Cotswolds or the Lake District are fortunate in that they may be able to assemble sufficient stones at little cost. The important thing to remember is that the wall-front should be on a batten, i.e. sloping slightly backwards from the base to the top, and that each stone should be tilted back as it is laid in place, packed with good soil, for you must remember that the soil can never be renewed short of taking the whole wall to pieces. If you can plant as you go, layer by layer, so much the better, for then the roots can be spread out flat instead of ramming them in later on, cramped, constricted, and uncomfortable. This method also enables you to vary the soil according to the requirements of its occupant: peat, or grit, can be added or withheld at will.

The top of the wall is full of possibilities. (I am assuming that your dry-wall is a retaining wall, built against a bank.) Not only can you fill it with things like *lithospermum* or pinks, or that pretty little rosy gypsophila called *fratensis*, to hang down in beards, on the wall-face, but a number of small bulbs will also enjoy the good drainage and will blow at eye-level where their delicate beauty can best be appreciated.

*   *   *

I can think of many small subjects for such a kingdom. The Lady-tulip, *Tulipa clusiana*, striped pink-and-white like a boiled sweet from the village shop, might survive for many more seasons than is usual in a flat bed. The little Greek tulip *orphanidea* would also be happy, in fact all the bulbs which in their native countries are accustomed to stony drought all through the summer. The dwarf irises would give colour in the spring, and their grey-green leaves would look tidy all the year round. Ixias, so graceful, for a later flowering. Lavender *stoechas*, which is all over these Spanish hills, should not damp off as it is apt to do in an ordinary border. This lavender would form agreeable clumps between the bulbs; fairly dwarf, it makes a change from the usual lavenders, such as the deep purple *nana atropurpurea*. Clip them close, when the flower-spike is going over, to keep them neat and rounded.

October 23, 1955

I wonder whether other amateur gardeners suffer the same grief and rage as I, on discovering that a certain plant which one had thought secure for years in its established place suddenly sickens, peters out, and dies? There must be some scientific reason, and I wish I knew it. I suspect, in my fumbling ill-informed way, that it has something to do with soil-exhaustion, meaning that a plant takes from the soil the nutriment it needs, and then won't thrive any longer after it has taken it. It is a well-known fact that the soil in which primulas have been grown for too long may become afflicted by what is called primula sickness; and this may well be the reason why other plants refuse to go on living and thriving in the same place year after year.

If I may quote examples from my own garden. I had, until last year, a stretch of Sweet Woodruff bordering a paved path under Kent cobnuts. Sweet Woodruff being one of our native, woodland plants, I imagined that it would go on happily for ever in the suitable conditions I had provided for it. Not so. It became black and spindly, and to all intent and purpose ceased to exist. I tried topping it up with some rich compost. No good at all. Compost was not what it craved for. But what did it crave for? How often one wishes that plants could speak, and how alarmed one would be if they did, much as Balaam must have been alarmed by his ass; however, I suppose one would get used to it; and how helpful it might be. 'Please could you supply me with some magnesium? I am deficient in chlorophyll, and my leaves are turning yellow. A few handfuls of magnesium would bring me round. A dose of Epsom salts might help. You haven't paid nearly enough attention to the trace-elements in my soil, and it is high time you did so.'

Another example from my own garden. For years past I have been growing polyanthus and coloured primroses under the same cob-nut trees. They used to be, if I may say so, a grand sight all through April and the first half of May. People came from far and wide to admire them. Last spring (1954) I noticed to my dismay that they were not as good and thick on the ground as usual. Even the seedlings I put out to fill up the gaps didn't thrive. Soil-exhaustion, I suppose; but what am I to do about it? I can't dig them all up and replant them somewhere else. Yet that is what they seem to demand. The Sweet Woodruff that has sown itself in other parts of the garden where I don't want it looks as green and healthy as the original plants.

It all seems to suggest that the ancient theory of rotation of crops may apply also to the pretty flowers we grow for our pleasure.

October 28, 1956

Topiary is a question on which opinions differ. Some people dislike seeing yew or box tortured into unnatural shapes; a tree, they contend, is a tree, not a pheasant or a rabbit or even a peacock or a tea-pot, and I suppose there is something to be said for their argument. Besides, topiary can so easily be overdone, when it becomes fussy and unrestful to the eye.

Other people, on the contrary, contend that clipped yew, properly used, adds greatly to the architectural design of a garden. Surely everyone will here be in agreement. We should stipulate, however, that the masses must be bold. The essential character of yew is its noble darkness, a darkness which gives solidity and throws into relief the more frivolous gaiety of the coloured flowers. Yew is grave and masculine. Let us therefore aim at heavy and sombre archways, or at huge balls and obelisks, and let it not be said that these demand the generosity of a large garden: many a modest garden would gain in dignity from their judicious use. How many small plots, for example, are divided between the flower garden and the kitchen garden; there must be a break, which could not be better accentuated than by a dark mysterious porch, never minding if it gives access only to the cabbages. Ah, you will say, yew is too slow of growth. Not so slow as most people suppose. True, it is far too slow for a temporary tenancy, but not too slow for any holding that is yours for life, when you can afford to think in terms of fifteen to twenty years. I planted a yew hedge in my own garden, and in fifteen years' time people assumed that it must be a century old. Expensive? Well, yes. Yew has gone up in price, to something like six shillings for a 2-ft. tree, but six trees would eventually grow into an archway as fat as could be desired.

Topiary has a very ancient history behind it, giving it a sort of traditional authority. The Romans practised it in great elaboration in their villas in Italy; and it is not too fanciful to suppose that when they settled in Britain and found our native yew ready to their hand, they employed it in their English villas as they had done at home. We may thus imagine the carefully trained peacock of our cottage gardens to come in direct descent from some homesick Roman legionary, a pleasing thought.

I saw recently an ingenious use made of an old yew hedge in a French garden. A section of it had been allowed to grow forward into the shape of a huge arm-chair. It looked so soft and comfortable that one was tempted to sink down into it. There was nothing fussy about this; it suggested only a large dark-green piece of furniture moved out of the house into the garden. With a little more ingenuity, one could have added a table in front of it, made out of one trunk or leg of yew with a flat clipped top.

October 30, 1955

My esteemed colleague, ex-nurseryman, and bold plant-collector, Mr. Clarence Elliott, renowned throughout the gardening world, apparently has an aversion to weeding. Not to weeding delicately and tactfully done by himself, but to the ruthless and indiscriminate extermination of all vegetation unrecognizable in its infant stage to the jobbing or indeed the professional employee. Groundsel and chick-weed, or seedlings of some precious primula, out they all come at the scrape of the hoe, and off they all go on to the rubbish heap together. This, as Mr. Elliott rightly remarks, effectively forfends desirable survivals. He has nothing good to say for so thorough a use of the hoe; he would prefer hand-weeding with his favourite tool, the widger. I some-times find myself bitterly in agreement with him. But one cannot hand-widge over more than a given area: time does not allow, so what is to be done about it?

One answer to the question is to go round the garden

oneself, putting a little stick beside any self-sown plant specially to be preserved.

I will give a practical example. That very ordinary but to my mind very beautiful *Cotoneaster horizontalis* sows itself all over the place, and chooses the oddest corners to sow itself in. Little dark-green herring-bone plants crop up everywhere, and seem to possess a special taste for putting themselves just where they will look best, but where we should never have dreamed of deliberately setting them. Such a small seedling appeared once at the right angle formed by a yew-hedge, and I let it grow, and now it makes a great fan of green and scarlet at the foot of the yew, a most unorthodox idea, abhorrent to any tidy-minded, hoe-wielding gardener, as Mr. Elliott would say, but oh, how dear to me!

It is something to have saved seedlings like this from destruction. I saved a lot more *Cotoneaster horizontalis*, 'rubbishy little things, only fit to be thrown away,' and planted them out on a sloping bank between azaleas. They have taken two or three years to make any show, but now they are fanning out and beginning to look fine under the flaming red foliage of the azaleas. On a wall opposite climbs a vine with huge red leaves, and above that a row of Sargent's cherry turns pink; it is all very ruddy and florid.

Incidentally, the cotoneaster is much to be commended as a ground cover for the discouragement of weeds, and, if you don't want a lot of wasps' nests in your garden, is a sumptuous collecting-ground for queen wasps when it comes into flower in May.

November

November 4, 1956

LAST Sunday (October 28, 1956, p. 168) in this column I was writing about topiary in the full expectation of reproachful letters saying that yew was too expensive and too slow of growth for the average garden-owner. So let me now revert to a cheaper and more rapid form of hedging which can be cut into shapes. It lacks the dark solemnity of yew, but it possesses a different charm of its own, in fact the French name for it is *charme*, meaning hornbeam.

Hornbeam is relatively cheap to buy, at 15s. a dozen for plants 2 to 2½ ft. high. It possesses an advantage for people who live on a chalky, limey soil, because like its botanical relation the beech it will put up with and will even enjoy an alkaline soil. Beech is more expensive, at £3 a dozen, and is also slower of growth. Both hornbeam and beech share the pleasant habit of retaining their brown leaves throughout the winter until the young green leaves come to poke their desiccated parents away in the spring.

Our friends and neighbours, the French, make a most imaginative use of hornbeam. They grow it into straight upright trees, with a trunk and then a level table-like top. They have fun with it, cutting and shaping it to whatever form desired. They may not be as successful with their flowers as we are, never having progressed far beyond the old Victorian system of bedding-out, but they certainly have a better sense of design than we, even though their straight lines and vistas may not invariably please the untidier and less disciplined English taste. I saw, however, a delightful use made of hornbeam, which seemed to combine severity of lay-out with a suggestive poetry in an enchanted garden at Fontainebleau. It was a perfect circle of hornbeam, perhaps 20 ft. high. a circle where every third tree had been omitted, but the tops allowed to join overhead, so that the whole ring was pierced at regular intervals, forming a kind of arcade through which glimpses of the surrounding garden could be surprisingly obtained. This effect of frame-work gave a sense of space and also provided a series of pictures, tempting the visitor to wander through and discover what lay beyond.

The old saying contains much truth. 'The Italians build their gardens, the English plant their gardens, the French design their gardens.'

November 6, 1955

One does not, in the southern provinces of France, pick up many ideas adaptable to northern gardens; the climate is too different, not only because many desirable plants would not be hardy with us, but also because the strong sunshine beautifies groups of colour which at home would look only too like the bedding-out of a municipal garden. Scarlet salvia, cannas, and even begonias glow with an intensity that gives them a new character.

I did, however, note a way of using one very ordinary plant, which at first sight I took to be our old friend the Virginia creeper,* *Ampelopsis veitchii*. I have always thought it a potentially very handsome thing in itself, as sanguine in autumn as any maple, but not when we behold it glued against the wall of a red brick villa. Here in the south I saw it growing free, tumbling in cascades over some terrace or clambering through some dark green tree, to fall

---

* How wrong I was; how unobservant. I should have remembered that the Virginia creeper was self-clinging, whereas this was a free loose rambling scrambling thing, with no sticky pads.

back in long loose strands of scarlet. Given its liberty it is
as startling as the red tropaeolum which ramps in Scotland,
but is often recalcitrant in England. I can imagine it wreathing a holly, or hanging amongst the branches of an ilex
(holm-oak) if you are so fortunate as to possess a fully
grown one, or even scrambling along a rough hedge of
thorn. Very often one finds such hedges with a holly left to
grow high, I believe because country people retain an old
superstition that it is unlucky to cut holly down to hedge-
level. However that may be, the sudden pyramid of scarlet
and green would flare like a torch, especially when caught
by the low rays of an autumnal sun.

I have laid emphasis on the advantage of some dark tree
as a host for the creeper, because to my mind the combination of dark green and brilliant red is one of the most
effective in nature, but I do recall once seeing a Virginia
creeper that had found its way high into the branches of a
silver birch. There it hung, pale pink and transparent in the
delicacy of the white tree. It must have been a garden
escape, for no one would have thought of planting it there,
on the edge of a wood.

The same idea could be extended to some of the ornamental vines, *Vitis coignettiae* for example, or *Vitis vinifera
brandt*. These have on the whole received better treatment
than the Virginia creeper. Not adhesive or self-clinging,
they have mostly been used over pergolas or archways,
when their beautiful rosy leaves could dangle at their
will, receiving the maximum of luminous light that they
crave and deserve. Not enough use is made of ornamental
vines in this country, nor have we learnt to grow them in
the way they can best be used, as I could imagine them
pouring loose and unrestricted, as I saw them treated, all
careless and rampant over the terraces and parapets of
ruined castle walls in my beloved corner of south-western
France.

November 11, 1956

From time to time an authoritative monograph comes out on some genus or plant-family, of the deepest value to the specialist and also of interest to the amateur. It tells the specialist all that he could want to know, and tells the amateur a good deal more than he can be bothered to cope with. The amateur should not be alarmed by such terms as cytology, morphology, clones, or chromosomes—basic numbers; he can skip these and can come down to what he really wants to learn about the history and cultivation of his favourite flowers.

In this case I am thinking about the snowdrops and the snowflakes. We all love snowdrops, with a sentimental love going back to our childhood. They bravely appeared through the snow, justifying their French name of *Perce-neige*, but perhaps we never knew very much about them beyond the fact that we could pick a bunch in January when there was very little else to pick.

Now if we want to learn more we can consult a book called *Snowdrops and Snowflakes*, by Sir Frederick Stern. Sir Frederick had begun it in collaboration with the late Mr. E. A. Bowles, two great experts coming together to produce a volume not likely to be superseded and full of information for the specialist and the amateur alike. I pick from its pages a few of the less technical facts which I always find so fascinating.

It is odd, for instance, that Shakespeare should never have mentioned the snowdrop, he who loved to bejewel his poetry with the names of our simple flowers. Yet the common snowdrop, *Galanthus nivalis*, may possibly be a native of Britain as well as having the widest geographical distribution, passing through Spain, France, Italy and the Balkans right into Russia. (It would be interesting to know if it ever grew, or still grows, wild in Warwickshire.) Sir Frederick suggests, very plausibly, that in Elizabethan times the snowdrop was known as the bulbous white violet, a name not very adaptable to poetry. Apparently it was never called snowdrop till fifty years after Shakespeare's death. It has been given other pretty names, such as White Ladies, Fair Maids of February and Candlemas Bells, but never the Milk Flower, although its botanical name, *galanthus*, derives from the Greek γαλα (gala), meaning milk. There are many varieties, and it may come as a surprise to learn that at least three are autumn-flowering, even so early as September. Personally I prefer my snowdrops at the accustomed time, in the depth of winter.

Cultivation is easy, though it must be remembered that the commonest form, *nivalis*, will do better in some localities than in others, notably in Scotland and the northern counties. I suppose everybody knows that the time to dig up and replant the bulbs, dividing the clumps if necessary, is when the flowers are just beginning to fade. Move them quickly, and do not let them come into contact with any animal manure: they hate it.

November 13, 1955

The problem of the small garden. I received a letter which went straight to my heart, more especially as it contained a plaintive cry that unintentionally scanned as a line of verse, 'I never shall adapt my means to my desires.' A perfectly good alexandrine, concisely expressing the feeling of millions, if not of millionaires.

The writer has a back garden 50 by 35 ft., and a front garden which he dismisses as being like any small villa in extent. How, he asks, would I harden my own heart if I had to decide between the demands of priority for the different seasons? Would I drop out one of the flowering periods altogether? No, I would not. I should always want at least one winter-flowering shrub, Witch-hazel for choice, and at least one tree of the cherry, *Prunus autumnalis subhirtella*, giving branches to pick from November till

March, and the yellow winter jasmine against a back wall of the house. Much use can be made of house-walls for climbers, without robbing any space from the garden proper. I should have little narrow beds running round three sides of the house, south, east and west, and these I should fill with bulbs of various kinds, dependent upon the taste of the owner, and dependent also upon the requirements of the bulbs, keeping the sun-loving kinds to the south, and kinds more tolerant of shade, such as snowdrops and winter aconites, to the east and west. I should cram my southerly bed with anemones, all opening to the sun, the blue Greek anemone *blanda*, the Italian blue *apennina*, and with the exquisite anemone *St. Bavo*, insufficiently grown yet so easy and self-sowing, of a beauty that far transcends the coarser blooms of *anemone St. Brigid* or even the handsome *anemone de Caen*. These narrow beds I should overplant with a variety of low-growing things, again dependent upon their choice of aspect, perhaps the creeping thymes to the south, making a red and lilac carpet of flower in late May and early June, perhaps the smaller violets to the east and west, but I should also leave spaces between them for the sowing of some chosen annuals, the blue cynoglossum and phacelia, also the Cambridge blue lobelia, and any other dwarf annuals as taste may dictate. These would make a summer display when the bulbs had died down, and would even persist into autumn if late sowings were made. On the north side, I would have foxgloves, of which many improved varieties are now obtainable.

This leaves the centre of the plot free for any bed or side border in which to grow flowering shrubs or herbaceous perennials. The boundary hedges I should unquestionably make of some flowering subject, since the wish of my correspondent is to prolong his season as far as possible. Some roses make an extremely effective hedge, the old striped *Rosa mundi*, for instance, or *conditorum*, more prettily known as *Assemblage des Beautés*; and there are evergreen kinds of berberis, flowering in spring and fruiting in autumn. It should thus be feasible, in the smallest plot, to cover the year and with ingenuity to do even better than I have suggested, by filling every odd corner with things like the September-October colchicums, the little pink and white cyclamen, too lowly to get in anybody's way, and some blue splashes of gentian if the soil is suitable.

November 18, 1956

Writing last Sunday, November 11, 1956, p. 174, about the snowdrops, I left myself no space to discuss the closely related snowflakes, or *Leucojum*. I don't think we grow the snowflake nearly enough. It is so graceful, being much taller than the snowdrop, its dangling bells rising 18 in. high through its rush-like leaves in April. May God forgive me, in my younger days I dug up a whole colony in a derelict garden I was trying to redeem; I didn't appreciate their beauty and recklessly moved them to an out-of-the-way corner where I am glad to say a few still survive. It was a particularly fine sample, in spite of being wickedly over-crowded, and should have been divided years before I ever came on it at all. These are the shocking things one does when one knows no better.

I know a bit better now, and would not be without *Leucojum aestivum*, especially the variety known as Gravetye. It flowers in April or May, which is rather misleading since *aestivum* means summer. *Leucojum vernum* is more true to its adjective, since it really flowers in spring, even as early as February or March, and is a very pretty thing for the rock-garden or for naturalizing in grass. It is a most obliging plant, since it will thrive either in sun or shade, and does not mind a limy soil. Like the snowdrop, it should be dug up and divided and replanted as soon as the flower begins to fade. This seems rather a strange thing to do,

when we are always told to let foliage of bulbs turn yellow
and die down before attempting to lift the bulbs at all.
Snowdrops and snowflakes work contrariwise. They like to
be lifted while they are still in full green leaf, broken up,
and reassembled in new young clumps.

Leucojum autumnale is rather a spindly-looking thing,
lacking the solidity of *vernum* and *aestivum*. It is said to be
hardy, but personally I do not feel tempted to bother about
it; one has these prejudices, and must abide by them. I do,
however, very strongly recommend the spring and so-called
summer snow-flakes, which are not very expensive at 8s.
and 10s. 6d. a dozen respectively and will give a good return
for your money in their yearly increase, as may be said of
most bulbs.

November 20, 1955

Will I please write an article on Lime-haters or What not
to waste Time on? My resolve to comply with this request
has been strengthened by a lament from a gentleman who
bought a *Pieris forrestii* last spring, planted it very carefully in the chalk of Epsom Downs, and is now surprised
to find it showing every sign of imminent collapse.

It is not possible to lay down any absolute and comprehensive law. There are some border-line plants which,
although happier on an acid (lime-free) soil, will still put
up with a certain degree of alkalinity. It is generally known,
I suppose, that most members of the vast Natural Order of
ericaceae are hostile to lime, thus imposing a serious limi-
tation on people who wish to grow rhododendrons, camellias,
azaleas, kalmias, andromedas, pernettyas, vacciniums, and
the majority of heaths and heathers; though even this large
family includes some members willing to oblige, *Rhododendron hirsutum* and *Rhododendron racemosum*, for
example, and *Erica carnea* among the heaths.

So no one need wholly despair. But at the same time my

first bit of advice to people determined to attempt things reluctant to thrive on an unsuitable soil would be: Don't. It is much better to stick to the things that happen to like the kind of soil you have got in your garden and give other things a miss. I know this is a hard saying, cutting out a whole lot of temptations, but I am sure it is a right one. It is no good trying to force plants to adopt a way of life they don't like: they just won't have it, unless you are rich enough to undertake excavations the size of a quarry. My second bit of advice would be: Make quite sure what type of soil you possess. There are various methods by which the amateur can make a test for himself, but only a rough estimate can be arrived at, and it is much better to bother a professional chemist. Any horticultural college or your county horticultural adviser will carry out the necessary test. If the sample is found to be acid or neutral, well and good: if it is found to be limy, you will have to proceed on a system of cautious elimination. There is a mysterious formula known as the pH scale: pH five and six are entirely acid and are the best for all working purposes; pH seven is neutral; and anything above pH seven is alkaline, or limy, and must therefore be regarded with suspicion.

As this is such an important subject, vital to the understanding of what to grow or not to grow, I shall return to it in a subsequent article. (See November 27, 1955, pp. 181–2.)

November 25, 1956

When I was recently motoring abroad, I observed two hedgerow trees, one in France and one in Spain. They puzzled me. They both had a leaf suggesting a *sorbus*, more familiarly known to us as Whitebeam or as the Rowan or Mountain Ash, or as the Service tree, but they carried clusters of fruit unlike any sorbus I had ever seen, in France like tiny red apples, in Spain like tiny brown pears. No doubt I ought to have been able to identify them, but one

cannot know everything, and as it turns out I was not
entirely at fault. They were indeed a form of sorbus, called
Sorbus domestica, and it was encouraging to learn that this
most decorative tree, although a native of central and
southern Europe, was sometimes to be found cultivated or
semi-wild in Britain; had been known to attain a height
between 60 and 70 ft.; and lived to the respectable age of
five or six hundred years.

It was less encouraging to learn that they should be
raised from seed, for this sounds a slow process where trees
are concerned. There seems to be an old theory that the
Service tree demands to be raised from seed, for John
Evelyn, writing in the seventeenth century, rather scoffs
at the idea that 'the sower never sees the fruit of his labour,'
and maintains that he himself has planted them as big as
his arm successfully and moreover that they 'come very
soon to be trees.' Evelyn, however, was not speaking of the
true Service tree, which apparently is the one I came across,
but of the *wild* Service tree, *Sorbus torminalis*, occasionally
to be seen in this country, a grand sight in autumn when
it turns red and gold. Evelyn was evidently ignorant of
Sorbus domestica, which is odd, because during his life-time
there was an already ancient specimen in Wyre Forest in
Worcestershire; probably he heard of it too late for inclusion
in his *Sylva*.

I shall try to grow *Sorbus domestica* from seed, in the
hope that my great-grandchildren may be grateful to me,
but meanwhile I would advise anybody to plant *Sorbus
hupehensis*, which can be bought as a young tree for about
7s. 6d. to half a guinea, * and is much to be recommended
for its faintly pink fruits, turning white as pearls, and the
autumn colouring of its leaves. It is of fairly recent
introduction from China, about 1910 I think, and is not yet

* From C. J. Marchant, whose address will be found on p. 195 of
this book.

often seen in our gardens. It makes a change from the usual red-berried rowan, so beautiful on wild hills amongst the heather, but sadly out of place on the front-lawn strip.

November 27, 1955

I hope that an article I wrote last week, November 20, 1955, pp. 178–9, on the difficulty of inducing lime-hating plants to grow in an alkaline soil did not spread alarm and despondency amongst those who happened to read it. It is true that they may have to forgo the pleasure of cultivating many favourites, but, on the other hand, there are two large categories about which no qualms need be felt. These categories comprise plants which positively require lime if they are to give of their best, and plants which negatively have no objection to its presence. In the first group, one has only to think of the native flora to be observed in calcareous districts: the beautiful spindle-tree brightening the hedgerows with its queer triangular fruits; the wild viburnum; the service tree, pure gold; the brooms; the gorse; the creeping thymes; the harebells; the sun-roses; the scabious; the stonecrops; and the now rare Pasque-flower, *anemone pulsatilla*. From these, and others, we may safely deduce that their garden relations will be delighted if we provide them with a limy home.

The second group is even larger. It includes the vast number of plants which will do well either with lime or without it. The great genus of the Rosaceae alone will carry us quite a long way. Many lilies (not all) are perfectly tolerant; in fact some of them, such as *L. henryii*, actively dislike the acidity of peat. Nearly all herbaceous plants are quite indifferent. Most irises are definitely calciphilous, if you like that word. As for trees and shrubs, the list is so long that it is quicker to refer back to the lime-haters mentioned in last Sunday's article, and to feel that you can safely go ahead with anything that does not occur in it; anything, that is, that the average gardener is likely to want.

Some rock-plants should be treated with caution, also some of the primulas and meconopsis. The lovely blue poppy, *Meconopsis betonicifolia* or Baileyi, which likes a spongy acid soil rich in peat and humus, is obviously not to be recommended to the chalk-dwellers. Of course, a certain amount can be done by taking out large pockets and filling them up with a more suitable mixture, but lime is extraordinarily persistent and seems always to return sooner or later, even a heavy rainfall will wash it back where it is not wanted, and perhaps enough has been said to show that the choice is wide and that there is no need to feel disheartened or discouraged.

December

December 2, 1956

THE fashion for indoor plants grows as rapidly as some of the plants recommended. This is understandable. Few of us have heated greenhouses now, so we must make the best use we can of the warm room and the sunny window-sill. We enviously remember the way our grandmothers kept their pots of scented geranium going for years, and a treasured pot of cyclamen, which, by all the rules, ought to have been chucked out on the rubbish-heap after its first or second flowering. I often wonder how our grandmothers managed so well, without all the helps and gadgets and advice now showered upon us.

I do not, myself, go in for indoor plants. I grow bulbs in fibre, as we all do, and am grateful for their successive gifts from Christmas onwards until the truly seasonal flowers begin to appear in the open garden. I don't really want to train strands of ivy over my bookshelves as our Scandinavian friends apparently do in Norway and Sweden; it would stop me from taking out the book I wanted.

All the same, there is one little indoor plant I would like to recommend to anybody who wants a bit of flourishing green in a pot or in a hanging basket. This is called *Tradescantia* in honour of Charles the First's gardener, John Tradescant. It is also known as the Wandering Jew or the Travelling Sailor, you can take your choice of the name. I think that both names must owe their derivation to the way this plant runs about in its roots: it roots at every node, and it throws out white worm-like roots, even if you keep a bit in water for a couple of weeks.

It is very pretty, with its green-and-white-striped leaves. I do wish that growers would not call it *trad*. These abbreviations are as distressing as daffs for daffodils, pollies for polyanthus, rhodos for rhododendrons, mums for chrysanthemums, glads for gladioli. One of the only abbreviations I like is a true country one: dandies for dandelions. But that is a child's word, not a nurseryman's.

To go back to house-plants, I would recommend a practical little book, *The Housewife book of house-plants*, by Xenia Field. Hulton Press, 8s. 6d. It will tell you all you want to know in simple comprehensive terms.

December 9, 1958

How comforting it is to feel that we still have at least three months before us in which to plant the shrubs we had forgotten. These after-thoughts can safely go in at any time up to next March, in fact most evergreens prefer to wait until the soil is likely to start warming up. This reflection gives us a sense of respite and reprieve.

One of the most charming small shrubs for the rock garden is *Syringa palibiniana*. I do resent having to call a thing syringa when what I really mean is lilac, but I cannot go against the dictum of my betters. *Syringa palibiniana*, from Korea, resembles what we should consider a miniature lilac, and the great point about it is its remarkable fragrance. Bury your face in its neat rounded top in May if you want to get all the distilled scent of every dew-drenched lilac you ever smelt. It comes high in the list of my garden darlings.

Perhaps I ought to qualify the term small or miniature shrub, since this is likely to lead to confusion. Most nurserymen who list it claim that it grows only to 3 ft. high. This is wrong, since in fact it will eventually grow to about 8 ft., a very different matter. Reputable nurserymen do not deliberately mislead their customers; leaving integrity apart, it would not pay them to do so. I think what has happened in the case of this syringa is that it starts to flower so profusely and at so young an age that a dwarf habit has been too rashly assumed.

What, then, are we to do? Obviously, we can't burden a small rock-garden with a shrub that intends to grow far taller than its companions or even than ourselves. There seems to be only one answer: plant it, enjoy it while it remains pigmy enough to share its place amongst other Lilliputians; and then when it gets above itself, dig it up and replant it in some open place where it can grow away to its Korean heart's content and let us see what happens.

I have, for the time being, put it amongst some daphnes of a similar round-headed type, Daphne *retusa* and *collina*, and have inter-planted them with a handful of the pink-and-white striped tulip *Clusiana*, the Lady-tulip. They should look pretty together, if only my scheme comes off. Alas, how seldom do these little schemes come off. Something will go wrong; some puppy will bury a bone; some mouse will eat the bulbs; some mole will heave the daphnes and the lilac out of the ground.

Still, no gardener would be a gardener if he did not live in hope.

December 11, 1955

Frost jumps suddenly upon us, and takes us unaware. We should not be unaware; we ought to know our climate well enough by now to be only too well aware of the dangers that may leap upon us between a sunset and a dawn. Yet how many gardeners take this threat in time? How many cover up their tender plants before it is too late?

I believe in shutting the stable door long before the horse has had a chance to get out.

These remarks may apply especially to the treatment of

shrubs or plants in large pots or wooden tubs. Many people grow hydrangeas or fuchsias in tubs, and are puzzled to know what to do about them through the horrible months we have ahead of us. Common sense tells us not to water them; water would simply congeal the soil into a block as hard as concrete. A far better plan is to wrap the pots round with any warm covering you can get, straw or bracken; or if your pots are not too large, sink them into a bed of ashes up to the rim. That will prevent the frost from getting at them, for of course you realize that a plant in a pot is far more vulnerable to frost than a plant in the ground. It has none of the protection of the deep surrounding earth, and must be artificially supplied by us with a deep, ashy sinking.

For the rest, what should one do for one's plants in pots? They are usually the most precious and treasured things. It is too large a subject to treat in so short an article, but generally speaking I would say this:—

Repot any plant which has become pot-bound. You can easily determine this necessity by seeing whether its roots are coming through the hole at the bottom.

If this does not seem necessary, scrape away the top-soil and give some fresh feeding, compost or bonemeal. Plants in pots naturally exhaust the soil they are planted in, and need replenishment. They have nothing else to draw on, and must depend upon us, their owners, for the nourishment they cannot obtain for themselves. Our responsibility is great towards these beautiful imaginations of Nature, so pathetically and helplessly at our command.

December 16, 1956

William Cobbett, in the intervals of rurally riding, wrote a now forgotten treatise called 'The English Gardener.' In it occurred a somewhat sour remark to the effect that 'the far greater part of persons who possess gardens really know very little about the matter and possess no principles relating to the art.' If the same could truthfully be said of us today, we should have no excuse for meriting the accusation. We are in the happy position of being able to visit hundreds of privately owned gardens, and also of having books showered upon us on every conceivable gardening subject.

From both these sources of information we should be able to pick up much guidance and many ideas. There is nothing nearer Learning-without-Tears than to walk round someone else's garden, making a note of the plants he is able to grow under natural conditions, and another note on happy effects of grouping and design, which we may not be ambitious enough to reproduce but at least may hope to adapt. Winter and petrol rationing forbid this occupation for the moment, so during the coming months we needs must take refuge in a fireside study of illustrated books that bring summer into our curtained rooms.

There are many such books today. A particularly alluring one has just been published, in good time for Christmas. It is called *English Gardens Open to the Public*, and when I say that it is published by Country Life and edited by Mr. A. G. L. Hellyer I must have said enough by way of recommendation. I lose my head completely when a book like this comes into my hands, spending a whole evening looking through the pages of photographs—those enviable lawns, those century-dark yew hedges, those calm pools, those woodland walks between silver birches, those distant views deliberately cut across our countryside, and the little manorhouses that so often make the background to an intimate, loved garden. It left me feeling that Cobbett was very much mistaken in saying that the greater part of persons who possess gardens really know very little about the matter. I thought that if Cobbett could come back in 1956 he would be astonished to see how much we had learnt and how many books we had consulted. He was writing long before the age of the photograph. We perhaps do not realize how much we owe to the photograph: we take it for granted now in 1956; we assume quite happily that it will bring gardens into our rooms in the long winter months before us. And perhaps Cobbett himself would acknowledge that our island can boast of the greatest number of the loveliest private gardens in the world.

December 18, 1955

The weeks between December 1st and January 1st are probably the most awkward from the point of view of the gardener who is asked to produce something to pick for the house. He, poor man, is expected to supply a succession of bunches and branches to enliven the rooms, especially over Christmas. His chrysanthemums are all over; and a good thing too, if they were those shaggy things the size of an Old English Sheepdog's face. The far lovelier Korean chrysanthemums went over long ago, unless he had facilities for keeping them under glass. He must fall back on the autumn-flowering cherry, on the winter jasmine, on *Viburnum fragrans*, on the berrying cotoneasters, on the waxy tassels and red fruits of *Arbutus unedo* if he had the foresight to plant one in his garden years ago. There is very little else that he can find except a few stray Algerian iris poking up through their untidy leaves.

I am in deep sympathy with this worried gardner, being a worried gardener myself, with a house clamouring for flowers when I haven't got any. Let me pass on a hint. It concerns the Christmas rose, *Helleborus niger*. If you happen to have an old clump in your garden, dig bits of it up and pot them into deep pots; put an inverted pot over each; keep them in the dark for a couple of weeks, and see what happens. You will find that the stalks are taller, and above all you will find that the flowers are of a purity and a whiteness they never achieved outside, not even under the protection of a cloche.

I know I shall be told that the Christmas rose does not like being disturbed. It is one of those plants with that reputation, but I am not at all sure that the reputation is wholly deserved. If you lift your clump with a large ball of soil, I guarantee that you will find it settling down again quite happily. It may not give of its best the first year, and for that reason it is advisable to stagger the potted clumps, some this year and some the next, planting them out into the open turn by turn.

December 23, 1956

It is well worth while, when putting the garden to bed for the winter, to search rather carefully for any stray seedlings which may have lain concealed beneath fallen leaves and the dead stalks of herbaceous stuff. It is surprising how many shrubs will thus reproduce themselves, even at some distance from their parent. They may be only a few inches high, when found, but by next spring they should start growing into useful little plants if you lift them with their roots intact and pot them up and sink the pots in a nursery row, either in ashes, sand, or ordinary soil. The point of sinking the pots is to safeguard them from getting frozen hard, as they would be if left standing nakedly in the open.

Many of the commoner shrubs, such as the berberis, the cotoneasters, the brooms, the hypericums and the buddleias, may often come to light in quantities and are just worth preserving if only to fill a gap in future or to give away.

I have also found more unexpected things than those: thriving little children of myrtle and the sweet-scented bay; the graceful indigofera; Clerodendron of the turquoise-blue berries; *Solanum crispum*, that energetic climber; and even self-sown yews which if only I had had the sense and foresight to regiment along a drill years ago would by now have developed into a neat clippable hedge.

This is all satisfactory enough, but there are even more exciting possibilities. There is the chance that one of these stray seedlings may turn out to be better than its parent, or at any rate different. I believe I am right in saying that *Rosa highdownensis*, that lovely hybrid of *R. moyesii*, appeared accidentally in Sir Frederick Stern's garden at Highdown, and that *Caryopteris clandonensis* of a deeper blue than either *Caryopteris mongolica* or *C. mastacanthus*, was suddenly noticed by the present secretary of the R.H.S. in his own garden at Clandon. Of course, to spot these finds you have to be endowed with a certain degree of serendipity, meaning the faculty of 'making discoveries by accident and sagacity' of something you were not deliberately in quest of.

This faculty involves knowledge, which is what Horace Walpole meant by serendipity when he coined his peculiar word. You have to know enough to recognize the novelty when you first see it, otherwise it might escape you altogether. You have to ensure also that the remorseless hoe does not scrape all your seedlings away into the heap destined for the barrow-load of rubbish. Scuffle about for yourself, before you let a jobbing gardener loose on beds or borders.

December 25, 1955

Writing last Sunday about flowers to pick for the house, I realized suddenly that never in the long course of these articles had I referred to the lily-of-the-valley-scented, winter-flowering berberis now known as *Mahonia japonica*. It is one of those plants which have undergone a change of name. It used to be called *Mahonia bealei*, and that is the name by which many nurserymen still offer it. *Mahonia bealei* appears to be only a distinct variety of *M. japonica*, slightly hardier, perhaps, stockier in growth and less strongly-scented, but if you want to get the real thing you will ask for *Mahonia japonica*.

It is a shrub highly recommendable if you have the right place for it. This does not mean that it is fussy as to soil. It likes a good loam, but does not object to some lime. What it really dislikes is a cold wind from the north or east, and who could agree more? We have those frightful months before us, when knives from the north and east cut through us, and we shiver and shudder and wonder if we have caught a chill. We can go indoors and get warm again, but our plants have to stand out in the cold, and do their best for us. We ought to be grateful to them, and I do feel grateful to the lily-of-the-valley-scented barberry that will endure some degrees of frost and will give me its yellow racemes of flower in January or February. It must have been very exciting for the plant-collector Robert Fortune, when he first discovered this treasure in Chusan Island so long ago as 1848. Now, it is a commonplace in our gardens.

It has the great advantage of being evergreen. It has the disadvantage of resenting transplantation. This means you must get it from a good nurseryman who will send it with a huge ball of soil, so that it scarcely notices that it has been dug up; but once you have got it established you will find that it pays a good dividend, year after year, in increasing value of scented racemes to pick for indoors.

May I please wish everybody a Happy Christmas?

December 30, 1956

The shortest day has passed, and whatever nastiness of weather we may look forward to in January and February, at least we can notice that the days are getting longer. Minute by minute they lengthen out. It takes some weeks before we become aware of the change. It is imperceptible even as the growth of a child, as you watch it day by day, until the moment comes when with a start of delighted surprise we realize that we can stay out of doors in a twilight lasting for another quarter of a precious hour.

There are things to pick. Not very many. One has to scrounge round, finding a berrying branch here and there, *Celastrus orbiculatus* for instance, exploding into the red and gold of its small fruits, so decorative that I wonder why people don't plant it to scramble up old trees or along rough hedges. The Christmas roses, *Helleborus niger*, are coming into flower now, and so is the winter jasmine, the yellow one, *Jasminum nudiflorum*.

We all know this jasmine. It is one of our stand-bys in the difficult months and is also one of the plants we think we can never treat so rough as to make it fail us. I protest that that is taking an unfair advantage of a most obliging friend. Thus we are told to grow it on a wall facing north, and indeed it is one of the few plants that will give without stint even in so dismal an aspect. Try it, however, in a position looking south, and note the difference in the gratitude of its golden showers. Then, again, we are instructed to cut it back violently after it has finished flowering. Docile, I followed this advice and chopped. My jasmine, which evidently knew better, has never yet recovered from the shock. (How often I regret that plants cannot talk.) Then, again, we have been taught to regard it as a climber. I don't believe it should be considered as a climber at all; at any rate, not artificially tied up to wires against a wall. I think it should be planted to pour down in loose masses from a tripod of 6-ft.-high posts lashed together into a point at the top. Unless, of course, you happen to have a terrace with a deep retaining wall for it to hang over like a curtain, which would probably suit it better than anything.

APPENDIX

Appendix

A SHORT LIST OF NURSERYMEN

FOR SHRUBS, TREES, FLOWERING TREES, CLIMBING PLANTS, ETC.

C. J. Marchant,
  Keeper's Hill,
    Stapehill,
      Wimborne, Dorset.

John Scott, & Co.,
  The Royal Nurseries,
    Merriott, Somerset.

Hillier & Sons,
  Winchester.

Burkwood & Skipwith,
  Park Road Nurseries,
    Kingston, Surrey.

George Jackman & Sons,
  Woking Nurseries,
    Woking, Surrey.

John Waterer Sons & Crisp, Ltd.,
  The Floral Mile,
    Twyford, Berkshire.

Robert Veitch,
  Exeter, Devon.

Treseder's Nurseries,
  Truro, Cornwall.

R. C. Notcutt,
  Woodbridge, Suffolk.
  (Lilacs a speciality.)

Arthur Charlton,
  Tunbridge Wells.

Winkfield Manor Nurseries,
  Ascot,
    Berkshire.

Donard Nursery Co.,
  Newcastle,
    Co. Down,
      Northern Ireland.

L. R. Russell,
  Richmond Nurseries,
    Windlesham, Surrey.

Sunningdale Nurseries (J. Russell)
  Windlesham, Surrey.

BULBS, CORMS, TUBERS, RHIZOMES, ETC.

Wallace & Barr,
  The Old Gardens,
    Tunbridge Wells,
      Kent.
  (Lilies, irises, and species tulips
    and crocuses a speciality.)

The Orpington Nurseries,
  Crofton Lane,
    Orpington, Kent.
  (For irises and Korean chrysan-
    themums.)

BULBS, CORMS, TUBERS, RHIZOMES, ETC.—*continued*

Walter Blom & Son, Ltd.,
   Coombelands Nurseries,
   Leavesden,
     Watford, Hertfordshire.

Alec Gray,
   Treswithian Daffodil Farm,
     Camborne, Cornwall.
   (Miniature narcissi a speciality.)

P. de Jager & Sons,
Windsor House,
London, E.C.4,
and 46, Victoria Street,
Westminster, S.W.1.

SEEDS

Thompson & Morgan,
   Ipswich, Suffolk.
   (A very long list, including many
     varieties not obtainable else-
     where.)

Sutton & Sons,
   Reading, Berkshire.

Carter's, Ltd.,
   Raynes Park,
     London, S.W.20.

W. J. Unwin, Ltd.,
   Histon, near Cambridge.

Ryder & Sons,
   St. Albans, Hertfordshire.

Thomas Butcher,
   Shirley,
     Croydon, Surrey.

Dobbie & Co.,
   Edinburgh, 7.

R. Bolton,
   Birdbrook,
     Near Halstead, Essex.
   (Sweet Pea specialists.)

Alexander & Brown,
   Perth.

ALPINES

W. E. Th. Ingwersen,
   Birch Farm Nurseries,
     Gravetye,
       East Grinstead, Sussex.

H. G. & P. M. Lyall,
   Mount Pleasant Lane,
     Bricket Wood,
       Watford, Hertfordshire.

H. Davenport-Jones,
   Washfield Nurseries,
     Hawkhurst, Kent.

Joe Elliott,
   Broadwell Nursery,
     Moreton-in-Marsh,
       Gloucestershire.

Jack Drake,
   Inshriach Alpine Plant Nursery,
     Aviemore,
       Inverness-shire.

C. Newberry,
   Bull Green Nursery,
     Knebworth, Hertfordshire.
   (Anemones a speciality.)

ALPINES—*continued*

Kuiper & Haskett,
  Kingsbridge, Devon.
  (Anemone specialists.)

A. R. & K. M. Goodwin,
  Stocklands Estate,
  Bewdley,
    Worcestershire.

Stuart Boothman,
  Nightingale Nursery,
  Maidenhead.

Robinson's Gardens Ltd.,
  60, North Park,
  Eltham, S.E.9.

FRUIT TREES—AND FRUIT IN GENERAL

Rivers,
  Sawbridgeworth,
  Hertfordshire.

Laxton Bros.,
  63H, High Street, Bedford.

GENERAL GARDEN STOCK—*Herbaceous plants*

It is not possible to give an exhaustive list, as most nurserymen who specialize in something or other usually carry a general list as well, but here are a few:

Baker, Codsall, Wolverhampton,
  (Russell lupins a speciality.)

Blackmore & Langdon Ltd.,
  Bath, Somerset.
  (Delphiniums and polyanthus a speciality.)

R. H. Bath,
  The Floral Farms,
  Wisbech, Cambridgeshire.

Kelway & Son,
  Langport, Somerset.
  (Peonies a speciality.)

Maurice Prichard & Sons,
  Riverslea Nurseries,
  Christchurch, Hampshire.
  (Many unusual plants.)

Bees Ltd.,
  Sealand Nurseries,
  Chester.

John Forbes,
  Buccleugh Nurseries,
  Hawick, Scotland.

Perry's Plant Farm,
  Enfield, Middlesex,
  (Water plants a speciality.)

ROSES

Edwin Murrell,
  Portland Nurseries,
  Shrewsbury.
  (Old-fashioned and species.)

T. Hilling & Co.,
  The Nurseries,
  Chobham,
    Woking, Surrey.
  (Old-fashioned and species roses.)

ROSES—*continued*

J. Russell,
    The Sunningdale Nurseries,
        Windlesham, Surrey.
    (Old-fashioned and species roses.)

Benjamin Cant & Sons,
    Old Rose Gardens,
        Colchester.

F. Ley,
    Windlesham, Surrey.

Wheatcroft Bros.,
    Ruddington, Nottingham.

H. Merryweather & Sons,
    Southwell,
        Nottinghamshire.

Daisy Hill Nurseries,
    (successors to T. Smith)
        Newry,
            Northern Ireland.

MacGredy & Son,
    Royal Nurseries,
        Portadown,
            Northern Ireland.

Archer & Daughter,
    Monk's Horton,
        Sellinge,
            Near Ashford, Kent.

HERBS

The Herb Farm,
    Seal,
        Sevenoaks, Kent.

Heath & Heather,
    Lullingstone,
        Eynsford, Kent.

HOUSE PLANTS

Wills & Segar,
    77, Old Brompton Road,
        London, S.W.7.

*Thomas Rochford & Sons,
    Turnford Heath Nurseries,
        Broxbourne, Hertfordshire.

* Wholesale, so orders must be placed through a retail florist.

ODDMENTS OF USEFUL ADDRESSES

The Royal Horticultural Society,
    Vincent Square,
        London, S.W.1.

Selective Weed-Killer, etc.
    Plant Protection,
        Yalding, Kent.

Hop-Manure
Wakeley Bros. & Co.,
    235, Blackfriars Road,
        London, S.E.1.

Sorbex Peat
Stuart Boothman,
    Nightingale Nursery,
        Maidenhead.

Cloches
Chase Protected Cultivation Ltd.,
    38, Cloche House,
        Shepperton,
            Middlesex.

ODDMENTS OF USEFUL ADDRESSES—*continued*

Labels
John Pinches,
   3, Crown Buildings,
     Crown Street,
      Camberwell,
       London, S.E.5.
   (Acme labels, metal.)

Sundries
Woodman & Sons,
   High Street,
     Pinner,
      Middlesex.

Wm. Wood,
   Taplow,
     Berkshire.